Sheet Metal
Machine Processes

Sheet Metal Machine Processes

CLAUDE J. ZINNGRABE • **FRED W. SCHUMACHER**

DELMAR PUBLISHERS
COPYRIGHT ©1975
BY LITTON EDUCATIONAL PUBLISHING, INC.

LIBRARY OF CONGRESS CATALOG CARD NUMBER: 73-2160

Printed in the United States of America
Published Simultaneously in Canada by
Delmar Publishers, A Division of
Van Nostrand Reinhold, Ltd.

DELMAR PUBLISHERS • ALBANY, NEW YORK 12205
A DIVISION OF LITTON EDUCATIONAL PUBLISHING, INC.

PREFACE

The fabrication of sheet metal ducts, fittings, and parts depends on the skill of the sheet metal technician in operating the machines of his trade. *Sheet Metal Machine Processes* not only explains the procedures used on hand-operated machines, but also those for power-operated machines.

This edition of the text has been up-dated and expanded to provide a step-by-step guide to the techniques of the sheet metal trade.

The following list summarizes the major features of *Sheet Metal Machine Processes*.

The performance objectives are listed at the beginning of each unit to indicate the desired student achievement upon completion of the unit.

The illustrations are closely correlated with the individual processes and show not only the various machines but also depict the proper procedures.

Sheet metal machine processes are described in a step-by-step fashion that is clear, concise, and easily understood.

The illustrations of the various tools include modern developments as well as those tools that have been used in the trade for many years.

Visual education is stressed for machine adjustment and operation.

The summary review questions provided are closely correlated to the unit content. These questions are provided at the end of each unit; answers to the review questions are provided in the Instructor's Guide.

Other texts in the Delmar Sheet Metal Technology series include:

Sheet Metal I, II, III, and IV

Sheet Metal Hand Processes

Practical Layout for the Sheet Metal Shop

Sheet Metal Blueprint Reading for the Building Trades

Mathematics for Sheet Metal Fabrication

Practical Problems in Mathematics for Sheet Metal Technicians

CONTENTS

The author and editorial staff at Delmar Publishers are interested in continually improving the quality of this instructional material. The reader is invited to submit constructive criticism and questions. Responses will be reviewed jointly by the author and source editor. Send comments to:

Director of Publications
Box 5087
Albany, New York 12205

MAR   1993

UNIT 1 *THROATLESS BENCH SHEARS – SLITTING SHEARS*

OBJECTIVES

After studying this unit, the student will be able to

- State the uses of the throatless shears and the slitting shears.
- Name the parts of the throatless shears and the slitting shears.
- List the adjustments of the blade on throatless shears and the slitting shears.
- Demonstrate the proper techniques for setting up and using the throatless shears and the slitting shears.

There are several types of shears used in the shop to cut sheet metal. The *scroll shears*, figure 1-1, is used for slitting and irregular contour cutting of 20-gage and lighter metal; the *rotary slitting shears*, figure 1-2, slits sheets up to 16 gage in thickness; the *cut-off shears*, figure 1-3, cuts off and slits sheet metal to a 16-gage thickness; the *lever shears*, figure 1-4, is used for slitting and irregular inside and out-side cutting of metal to a thickness of 12-gage mild steel. The throatless bench shears is shown in figure 1-5. The most commonly used machines are the throatless bench shears and the slitting shears.

Fig. 1-1 Scroll shears   **Fig. 1-2 Rotary slitting shears**

THROATLESS BENCH SHEARS

The throatless bench shears, figure 1-5, is an all-purpose cutting machine. The throatless shears will cut heavy metal up to a 3/16-inch thickness without distortion. The operating principle of these shears is the same as that of a pair of snips except that the shears has a compound leverage action for greater power. Because of the curved blade design, the work can be turned in any position while it is being cut.

Parts

The throatless shears consists of a bed, handle, hold-down adjustment, two cutting blades, blade clamps, and several adjustment screws, figure 1-5.

Fig. 1-3 Cut-off shears   **Fig. 1-4 Lever shears**

Figures 1-1 – 1-4 courtesy of The Peck, Stow, & Wilcox Co.

1

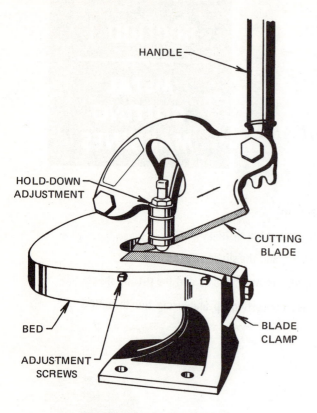

Fig. 1-5 Throatless bench shears

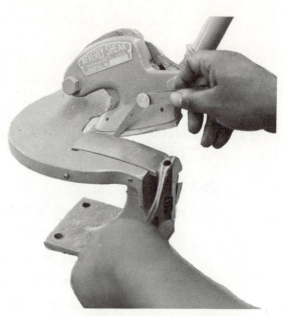

Fig. 1-6 Adjusting for blade clearance

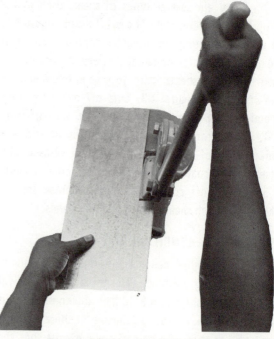

Fig. 1-7 Adjusting cutting line to blade

Blade Clearance

The required blade clearance is obtained by adjusting the lower blade on the shears, figure 1-6. The allowance for a burr-free cut can be made by setting the blade clearance at 1/10th the thickness of the metal to be cut. The following procedure is to be used to make the blade clearance adjustment.

1. Loosen the blade clamp, figure 1-6.

2. Tighten or loosen both adjustment setscrews until the desired blade clearance is obtained. Check the blade clearance with a feeler gage.

3. Make a test cut and examine the cut edges for burrs. If burrs are present, correct the adjustment or have the blades sharpened.

4. Tighten the blade clamp.

5. Raise or lower the hold-down screw (on heavier-gage models only), so that the ball bearing is in firm rolling contact with the work.

    Note: All moving parts of the throatless shears are to be kept well oiled with a good grade of machine oil. Use a good graphite oil on the insides of the blades.

HOW TO USE THE THROATLESS SHEARS

1. Open the shears as wide as possible by lifting the handle upward, figure 1-7.

Fig. 1-8 Slitting shears

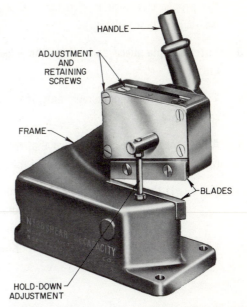

Fig. 1-9 Slitting shears (Courtesy of Whitney Metal Tool Co.)

2. Place the stock to be cut on top of the lower blade so that the scrap portion of the stock is under the upper blade. The portion under the upper blade will curl and be distorted as a result of the cutting action.

3. Adjust the cutting line on the stock so that it is in line with the top blade.

4. Adjust the hold-down screw so that the ball bearing makes firm contact with the work.

5. Make the first cut by pulling the handle down.

   Note: If a curved pattern is to be cut, adjust the stock with the left hand so that the stock follows the cutting action of the upper blade.

6. Repeat steps 1 to 3 and 5 until the entire pattern is cut.

SLITTING SHEARS

The slitting shears, figure 1-8, is used for the straight slitting, notching, and trimming of sheet metal of thicknesses up to 3/16 inch. The slitting shears is designed so that sheet metal can be slit to any length or width. A compound leverage action provides greater power and ease of cutting.

Parts

The slitting shears consists of a frame, upper and lower blades, handle, hold-down adjustment, and adjustment and retaining screws, figure 1-9.

Blade Clearance

The required blade clearance is obtained by adjusting the lower blade on the shears. The blade clearance should be maintained at .000 to .002 inch for all thicknesses of metal up to the rated capacity of the shears. The following procedure is to be used to make the blade adjustment.

1. Loosen the retaining screws, figure 1-9.

2. Tighten or loosen the three headless adjustment screws that bear against the lower blade until

Fig. 1-10   Scrap curls down when cut with slitting shears

the proper clearance is obtained. Check the clearance with a feeler gage.

3. Cut a sample piece and check the edges for burrs.

4. Tighten the retaining screws only if the cut is satisfactory.

5. Adjust the hold-down screw so that the material being cut lies flat on the bed of the shears.

    Note: If the blades are sharpened to compensate for wear, raise the lower blade by adjusting the retaining screws in their elongated mounting holes. Keep all

moving parts of the shears oiled with a good grade of machine oil.

HOW TO USE THE SLITTING SHEARS

1. Open the shears as wide as possible by raising the handle..

2. Place the piece to be cut under the blade with the scrap portion to the right of the blade, figure 1-10, page 3.

3. Line up the cutting line with the top blade edge.

4. Adjust the hold-down screw.

5. Make the first cut by lowering the handle.

6. Repeat steps 1 to 3 until the cut is complete.

SUMMARY REVIEW

A. Place your answers to the following questions in the column to the right.

1. State two general uses for a throatless shears.

    1. _____
    _____

2. Name the parts of a throatless shears.

    2. _____
    _____
    _____
    _____
    _____
    _____
    _____

3. List the two general adjustments that should be made on a throatless shears.

    3. _____
    _____

4. State three general uses for the slitting shears.

    4. _____
    _____
    _____

5. List the parts of the slitting shears.

    5. _____
    _____
    _____
    _____
    _____
    _____

6. What are the two general adjustments that can be made on a slitting shears?

    6. _____
    _____

B.   Insert the correct word or phrase in the following:

1.   The capacity of a throatless shears is usually _____ .

2.   A setting of _____ the stock thickness is the approximate blade clearance on a throatless shears.

3.   The blade clearance on a slitting shears should be set at _____ to _____ inch.

4.   Ease in cutting with a slitting shears is due to its _____ action.

C.   Underline the correct word or phrase in the following:

1.   The scrap metal should (curl down, curl up, remain straight) during the cutting action on a throatless shears.

2.   The ball bearing of the hold-down adjustment on the throatless shears should (remain free, touch, firmly contact) the metal.

3.   The capacity of a slitting shears generally is (16 gage, 1/8 inch, 3/16 inch, 20 gage).

4.   The blades of a slitting shears are adjusted for (all gages, each gage, several gages) of metal at one time.

UNIT 2 SQUARING SHEARS

OBJECTIVES

After studying this unit, the student will be able to

- List the uses of the squaring shears.

- List materials that can be cut on a squaring shears.

- Name the parts of a squaring shears.

- List the safety precautions to be taken when operating a squaring shears.

- Set and adjust all gages.

- Demonstrate the proper procedure for cutting and squaring a sheet.

Sheet metal can be cut by hand or by machine. The machine method is quicker and more accurate.

There are several types of machine shears; the squaring shears is used most frequently. The *squaring shears,* figure 2-1, is used to trim or make straight cuts on sheet metal and to cut sheets so that the sides are square. Squaring shears are equipped with *gages* which are used as stops for the sheets when more than one piece of the same size is required. This type of shears is used to cut various kinds of sheet metal such as tinplate, galvanized iron, black iron, zinc, copper, aluminum, and stainless steel.

SQUARING SHEARS

The squaring shears consists of a bed, two housings, a crosshead, a hold-down attachment, a

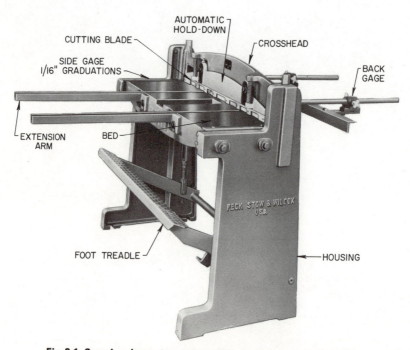

Fig. 2-1 Squaring shears (Courtesy of The Peck, Stow & Wilcox Co.)

foot treadle, two cutting blades, and several gages, figure 2-1.

The lower cutting blade is fastened to the bed which supports the sheet while the sheet is being cut. A deep groove is cast in the face of the bed to permit easy removal of the sheets. Slots are provided in the bed so that the front gage can be clamped to the face of the bed. If wide sheets are to be cut, the front gage is fastened to extension arms which are bolted to the bed.

The upper blade, which is fastened to the crosshead, is operated by stepping on the foot treadle. This blade is set at a slight angle to the lower cutting blade. As a result, the blades cut only a small part of the material for each cut. Thus, the surface area cut each time is reduced and the force necessary to make each cut is reduced, figure 2-2.

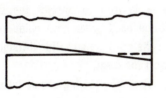

Fig. 2-2

The standard sizes of foot-operated squaring shears vary from a 22-inch to 120-inch length of cut; these shears will cut 16-gage mild steel. Power-driven machines are available and will cut metal of all gages with lengths of cut from 30 inches to 120 inches. The power-driven machines reduce fatigue and save time.

A squaring shears with open housings is called a *gap shears*, figure 2-3. Using the gap shears, it is possible to shear sheets that are longer than the cutting length of the shears by making successive cuts. These shears are available in 36-inch to 72-inch standard cutting lengths and have an 18-inch gap in the housings. The size of the gap limits the width of the cut to 18 inches.

Safety Precautions

A guard should be installed on every squaring shears to prevent the operator's fingers from coming in contact with the cutting blades. In general, shears are not provided with guards as standard equipment; therefore, when new shears are delivered to the customer, guards must be installed. According to the New York State Industrial Code (Bulletin #19), the distance between the lower edge of the guard and the

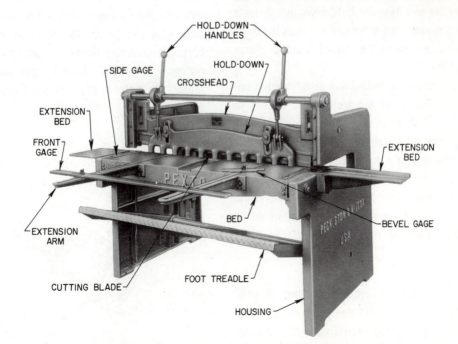

Fig. 2-3 Gap squaring shears (Courtesy of The Peck, Stow & Wilcox Co.)

bed of the shears should not be more than 3/8 inch. One type of guard, the *See-thru Finger Guard*, enables the operator to see the edge of the lower cutting blade.

One sheet at a time can be cut on the squaring shears. Wire, rod, bar stock, seamed edges, grooved, or welded metal must not be cut on this machine. Squaring shears are never used to cut materials of any size which exceed the capacity of the machine. The bed of the shears must be cleaned before any cutting is done. The squaring shears should be lubricated periodically.

The material generally is inserted from the front of the machine. With long sheets, it is more convenient to insert the material from the rear of the machine as this allows more freedom when operating the foot treadle.

One person normally can operate the squaring shears. The cut is completed and the foot treadle released before the metal is picked up from the rear of the machine. If an assistant is necessary, the operator must make certain that the assistant's hands and feet are clear of the machine before stepping on the foot treadle.

Description and Use of the Hold-Down Attachments

There are two kinds of hold-down attachments for squaring shears: one attachment clamps the sheet automatically, and the other type is used to clamp the sheet by hand.

A hand-operated, hold-down attachment is operated independently of the treadle and is used to clamp the metal sheet in place before cutting. This attachment prevents the sheet from moving while it is being cut, resulting in a more accurate cut. On some machines the foot treadle automatically clamps the sheet before the cut is made. This feature enables the cut to be made more rapidly and is usually found on shears used for light-gage material.

Side Gages

The *side gages* are rectangular bars of steel bolted to the bed. The upper face of each bar contains a scale graduated in 1/16-inch intervals with markings from 0 to 14 inches for cutting material to a certain width. The edge of the sheet to be cut is pressed against the gage when a cut at right angles to the edge is desired.

Back Gage

The *back gage*, figure 2-1, consists of an angle iron bolted to two brackets which slide on two rods fastened to the rear of the machine. The top of each rod is marked with a scale from 0 to 28 inches graduated in 1/16-inch intervals. The bottom of the rod is a rack on which a pinion adjusts the sliding brackets to any cutting distance desired. A screw clamp, located on the inside of the sliding mechanism, locks the gage at the required cutting distance. This gage is used primarily when narrow pieces of metal are to be cut. If wide pieces of light metal are to be cut and the rear gage is used, an assistant must hold the sheet against the angle iron to prevent the sheet from sagging. Some back gages have guide rods which extend from the machine and slide through the angle iron to support the sheet.

Some types of squaring shears have a special *dial-set back gage*, figure 2-4. A dial with graduated intervals of 1/64 inch is used to set this gage. The gage is locked in place by means of a plunger which will vary the setting by only 1/128 inch. The dial-set back gage can be set for either parallel or angular cutting by rotating the locking plunger to the desired setting. Some dial-set back gages are moved by a motor; the distance of travel is indicated at the front of the machine.

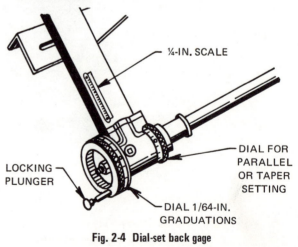

Fig. 2-4 Dial-set back gage

Fig. 2-5 Correct position of hands and feet while cutting on foot-operated shears

Fig. 2-6 Proper position of sheet while squaring

Fig. 2-7 Marked sheet held in place for cut

Front and Bevel Gages

The *front gage* is a rectangular bar with two slotted holes. It is attached to the machine by two bolts which slide in elongated holes in the bed. It also can be attached to the extension arms bolted to the bed, figure 2-1. The gage is used when more than one piece is required.

The *bevel gage* is a short bar with one hole. It can be attached to the shears with a bolt through either slot in the bed, figure 2-1. This gage is used alone or with the front gage when the edges of many sheets are to be cut at an angle.

HOW TO SQUARE A SHEET

1. From the front of the machine, insert the sheet to be cut between the cutting blades.

   a. When squaring a sheet, place it on the left side of the squaring shears; this location reduces the possibility of the sheet moving while it is being cut.

   b. Most of the sheet should rest on the bed of the shears.

2. Extend the edge to be trimmed about 1/8 inch beyond the lower cutting blade; this distance should never be less than the thickness of the sheet being cut.

3. Pull the hold-down handle to clamp the sheet in place.

4. Keep both hands on the sheet and step on the foot treadle to make the cut, figure 2-5.

   CAUTION

   Be sure that your fingers are away from the cutting blades; do not reach behind the machine while stepping on the foot treadle.

5. Release the foot treadle gradually, keeping your foot on the treadle until it reaches its original position.

6. Release the hold-down handle and remove the sheet.

7. Place the cut edge of the sheet against either side gage, figure 2-6.

8. Push the sheet between the blades so that the metal extends about 1/8 inch beyond the lower blade.

9. Hold the sheet against the side gage with one hand and pull the hold-down handle with the other hand.

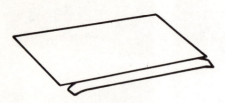

Fig. 2-8 Sheet with edges bent

10. Make the cut, release the hold-down handle, and remove the sheet.

11. To square the other side of the sheet, repeat steps 7 to 10.

HOW TO CUT A MARKED SHEET

1. Place the sheet so that the line to be cut is flush with the edge of the lower cutting blade; check the alignment by looking down between the hold-down and the upper cutting blade. Pull the hold-down handle, figure 2-7, page 9.

   Alternate Method: Make a 1/2-inch notch with hand snips at each end of the marked line; bend down both notches, figure 2-8. Place the sheet on the bed of the squaring shears from either the front or back of the machine with the greater part of the sheet on the bed; then draw the sheet with the bent edges against the lower blade of the shears. Pull the hold-down handle.

2. Make the cut, release the hold-down handle, and remove the sheet.

HOW TO CUT SHEETS USING THE FRONT GAGE

1. Place both ends of the front gage at the desired graduation on the side gage, or, set the gage by measuring with a rule from both ends of the gage to the cutting edge of the lower blade, figure 2-9.

2. Tighten both front gage bolts with an open wrench. The gage must not move while the bolts are being tightened.

3. Insert the sheet between the cutting blades from the front of the machine; 1/8 inch of the sheet should rest on top of the front gage. Hold the sheet against the left side gage, figure 2-10.

4. Pull the hold-down handle and make the cut.

5. Release the hold-down handle and turn the sheet end for end. Place the cut edge against the front gage.

6. Pull the hold-down handle and make the cut.

   Note: If the sheet is to be squared on four sides, hold the cut edges against the side gage and square as before.

HOW TO CUT SHEETS USING THE BACK GAGE

1. Set the back gage by adjusting the sliding brackets to the desired length as indicated on the scale of the sliding arms. Lock the gage in position.

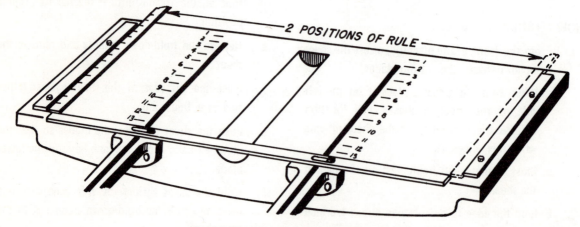

Fig. 2-9 Checking the front gage with a rule

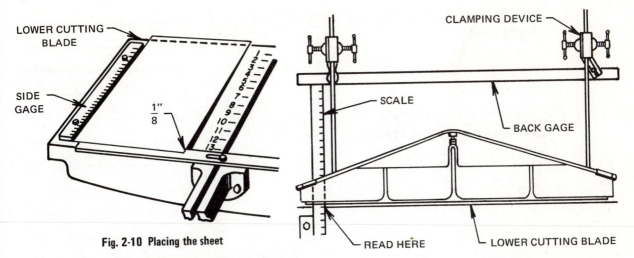

Fig. 2-10 Placing the sheet

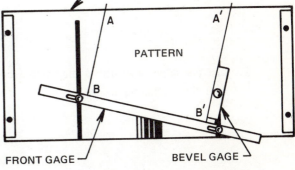

Fig. 2-11 Setting the back gage

a. After setting both ends of the back gage, recheck both ends of the gage with a scale, figure 2-11.

b. If the squaring shears has a special dial-set back gage, set the gage with the locking plunger as shown in figure 2-4, page 8.

2. Trim the front edge of the sheet with the squaring shears.

3. Push the sheet between the cutting blades until the trimmed edge is against the back gage and pull the hold-down handle. The sheet must be level with the bed to insure accuracy.

4. Make the cut, release the hold-down handle, and remove the sheet.

HOW TO CUT A SHEET USING THE FRONT GAGE AND THE BEVEL GAGE

1. Place the pattern on the bed of the squaring shears.

2. Move the pattern so that edge AA' is flush with the lower cutting blade, figure 2-12.

3. Pull the hold-down handle to hold the pattern in place.

Fig. 2-12 Setting the front and bevel gages

4. Set the bevel gage flush with side A'B' of the pattern and tighten the bevel gage.

5. Set the front gage flush with edge BB' of the pattern and tighten the front gage.

6. Release the hold-down handle, remove the pattern, and place the sheet to be cut against the front gage and the bevel gage.

7. Pull the hold-down handle and make the cut.

SUMMARY REVIEW

A. Place your answers to the following questions in the column to the right.

1. Name the two general uses for the squaring shears.

1. _____

_____

2. Name the materials in sheet form that can be cut on the squaring shears.

2. _____
    _____
    _____
    _____
    _____

3. List all the parts of a squaring shears.

3. _____
    _____
    _____
    _____
    _____
    _____
    _____
    _____

4. State four materials that should not be cut on a squaring shears.

4. _____
    _____
    _____
    _____

5. List the safety precautions that should be taken when operating a squaring shears.

5. _____
    _____
    _____
    _____
    _____

B. Insert the correct word or phrase in the following:

1. A squaring shears with an open housing is called a _____ .

2. Metal that has been cut is picked up from the _____ of the shears.

3. Cutting with a hold-down attachment on the squaring shears is more _____ .

4. When a cut at right angles to the sheet edge is to be made, the _____ gage is used.

5. The _____ gage is used in cutting a series of small pieces.

C. Underline the correct word or phrase in the following:

1. The general practice is to insert the material from the (back, front, side) of the shears.

2. The capacity of a standard size foot-operated squaring shears is (14, 16, 18, 20, 26) gage.

3. The edge of a sheet to be trimmed should extend about (1/16, 1/8, 1/4, 1/2) inch beyond the lower cutting blade.

4. In cutting large pieces of metal using the back gage, sagging will cause (injury, damage, inaccuracy).

5. The face of the side gage of a squaring shears is marked in fractions from 1 to 14 inches in (64ths, 32nds, 16ths, 8ths).

UNIT 3 *RING AND CIRCLE SHEARS*

OBJECTIVES

After studying this unit, the student will be able to

- Name the two types of circle-cutting shears.
- List the parts of the ring and circle shears.
- List the adjustments on the ring and circle shears.
- Demonstrate the proper techniques for cutting a ring, a circle, and a curve.
- Slit a sheet on the ring and circle shears.

Circle-cutting machines are used where circular pieces must be cut accurately from sheet metal. Two types of circle-cutting machines are shown in figure 3-1, the *circle shears*, and figure 3-2, the *ring and circle shears.* The upper cutter of the circle shears cannot be moved, so the only cuts that can be made must start from the outside edge of the sheet, such as outside circles. The upper cutter of the ring and circle shears can be raised and lowered to allow the cutting of circles inside blanks and rings. Both machines can be used for slitting sheets and making irregular cuts. The ring and circle shears is preferred in the shop because of the variety of cuts it can make. The circle shears, figure 3-1, will cut circles of diameters ranging from 3 to 48 inches from square blanks. The capacity of the circle shears is 22-gage mild steel.

RING AND CIRCLE SHEARS

The ring and circle shears, figure 3-2, page 14, will cut circles varying in diameter from 3 1/4 inches to 42 1/2 inches from square blanks. The capacity is 20-gage mild steel. Both power-driven and hand-operated machines are manufactured with the capacity to handle large-diameter circles and heavier than 20-gage metal.

Parts

The ring and circle shears consists of a bed, a cutting head with two rotary cutters, and a sliding circle arm with discs to hold the blank while it is being cut, figure 3-2, page 14.

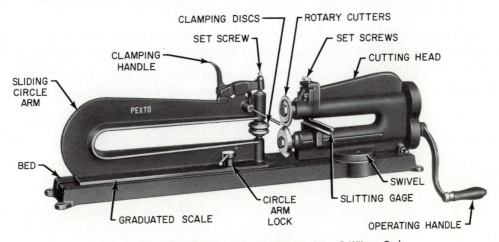

Fig. 3-1 Circle shears (Courtesy of The Peck, Stow & Wilcox Co.)

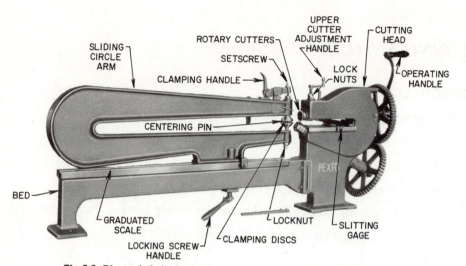

Fig. 3-2 Ring and circle shears (Courtesy of The Peck, Stow & Wilcox Co.)

Adjustments

The *cutting head* contains two rotary cutters which are connected by gears and rotated by an operating handle. The upper cutter can be raised or lowered by turning an adjustment handle located above the cutter. The distance that the upper cutter can be lowered is set by two locknuts which allow the operator to stop the upper cutter at the same position for each cut, thus insuring uniform cuts. The lateral clearance between the cutters is obtained by adjusting the lower shaft. For light materials, the cutters should just touch but they should not rub against each other. For heavy materials, the cutters should be separated slightly. The cutter adjustment is made according to the manufacturers' instructions.

The *sliding circle arm* has two clamping discs mounted in the open end of the throat, figure 3-2. A clamping handle adjusts the upper disc so that the sheet is held firmly between the two discs. The height of the discs and the pressure they exert on the metal blank is controlled by adjusting a setscrew and a locknut. The lower disc has a removable centering pin for finding and then holding the center of the blank while the cut is being made.

When the zero marks on the swivel base line up, the cutting head is set slightly off center toward the operator, figure 3-3. This is the proper setting to obtain clean cuts and true circles when cutting metal of thicknesses up to the capacity of the machine. To cut very small circles, the cutting head may be set even more off center. The swivel base is clamped in place with locking bolts. Each setting is checked by running a piece of scrap metal through the machine. When the cutting head is set properly, the blank feeds freely and easily without strain on the clamping discs.

The blank rotates about the center of the clamping discs while the cutters follow a circular course, feeding the material automatically toward the operator until the cut is completed.

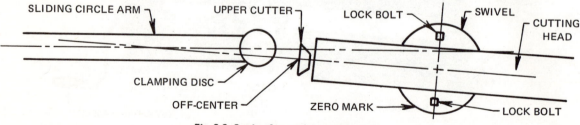

Fig. 3-3 Setting for cutting outside circle

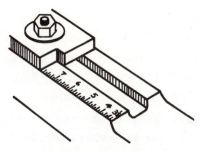

Fig. 3-4 Graduations on the bed

The Graduated Scale

A graduated scale divided into 1/8-inch intervals, figure 3-4, is located on the upper side of the bed. The setting of the circle arm on this scale determines the diameter (not the radius) of the circle being cut. A mark on the sliding circle arm is used to line up the arm with the scale on the bed.

The Slitting Gage

The *slitting gage* is a movable arm attached to the bed of the shears by a bolt, figures 3-1 and 3-2. The gaging surface can be replaced when it is worn. The slitting gage is used to make straight cuts parallel to the edge of a sheet. The position of the gage determines the cutting width of the metal.

There are two methods of cutting circles. In the first method, the circle is scribed on the blank with dividers and the sliding circle arm is set for this circle; for the second method, the sliding circle arm and the sliding gages are set to cut the circle. The circle is not laid out on the blank if this method is used. The former method is the more accurate and practical way to cut circles.

To produce true circles and clean cuts, the cutters and the sliding circle arm must be set correctly and the clamping discs must be level with the cutters. The settings should be checked on a piece of scrap metal before the job is started.

Machine Maintenance

The machine should be lubricated at regular intervals. The manufacturer's instruction sheet is to be consulted for information regarding the oiling and adjustment of the machine.

Fig. 3-5 Centering and clamping the blank

HOW TO CUT A CIRCLE

1. Prick punch the center of the square blank.

    Note: The centers of square or rectangular blanks can be found by drawing lines from opposite corners (diagonal lines between the corners); the point of intersection is the center of the blank.

2. Scribe the required circle on the blank with a pair of dividers. The graduated scale on the bed can be used to set the sliding circle arm if the sheet metal worker does not wish to scribe the circle on the blank.

3. Turn the blank over and prick punch the center point from the opposite side.

4. Set the locknuts on the upper adjustment handle so that the upper cutter in its lowest position produces a clean cut.

5. Raise the upper cutter using the adjustment handle.

6. Hold the blank in your right hand; then, place the prick punch mark on the center point of the lower clamping disc with the scribed circle upward, figure 3-5.

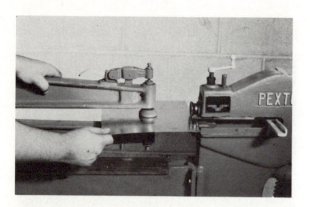

Fig. 3-6A Setting the circle arm

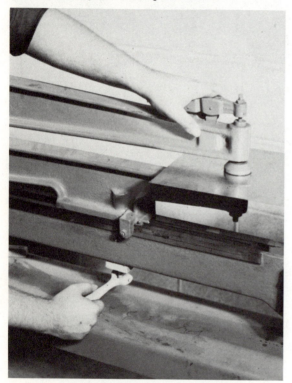

Fig. 3-6B Locking circle arm in position

Note: The blank should be level with the cutter when it is clamped in place; do not clamp the blank too tightly as this will ruin the cutters. The position and the pressure of the clamping discs can be adjusted by the setscrews and locknuts above and below the clamping discs.

7. Clamp the blank in place by pushing the clamping handle down with the left hand, figure 3-6A.

8. Use a wrench to loosen the locknut on the sliding circle arm, figure 3-6B.

9. Slide the circle arm so that the edge of the scribed circle on the blank is flush with the cutting edge of the upper cutter.

Note: If the circle is not scribed on the blank, use the graduated scale on the bed to set the sliding circle arm. Check the accuracy of these graduations by setting the sliding circle arm on one of the inch graduations. Then, measure with a scale from the cutting edge of the upper cutter to the center of the clamping discs, figure 3-7. The scale reading should be one-half the graduation reading on the bed.

10. Tighten the locknut on the circle arm.

11. Turn the blank by hand to insure that the cutters are in line with the scribed circle on the blank.

12. Lower the upper cutter, figure 3-8. For heavier metals, turn the operating handle slightly while lowering the upper cutter.

13. Turn the operating handle with the right hand until the circle cut is complete, figure 3-9.

CAUTION Do not allow long hair to hang freely, and do not wear loose clothing while working on the machine. Keep fingers away from the cutters.

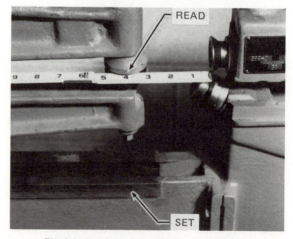

Fig. 3-7 Checking the graduations on the bed

Fig. 3-8 Adjusting the upper cutter.

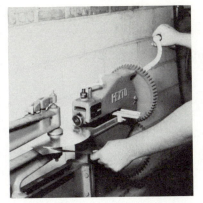

Fig. 3-9 Cutting a disc

Fig. 3-10 Cutting a ring

14. Release the clamping handle and remove the disc.

HOW TO CUT A RING

Follow steps 1 to 12 of the procedure "How To Cut A Circle" to cut the outer circle. Raise the upper cutter, loosen the lock on the sliding circle arm, and then slide the circle arm forward using either the scale on the bed or the inner scribed circle to determine the correct position. Tighten the lock on the circle arm, lower the upper cutter, and cut the inner circle, figure 3-10.

HOW TO SLIT A SHEET

1. Set the slitting gage by measuring with a rule from the upper cutting edge a distance equal to the desired width of the piece in the recess of the slitting gage. In figure 3 -11, the gage is being set for 5 inches.

2. Set the upper cutter and begin the cut. Feed the sheet with the left hand while the edge of the sheet is held against the slitting gage, figure 3-12.

CAUTION When cutting long pieces or many short pieces, the material should be fed towards the operator by another worker to prevent the cutters from loosening.

How to Make Irregular Cuts

Set the upper cutter and feed the material slowly, while moving the sheet so that the upper cutter follows the layout line.

Fig. 3-11 Setting the slitting gage

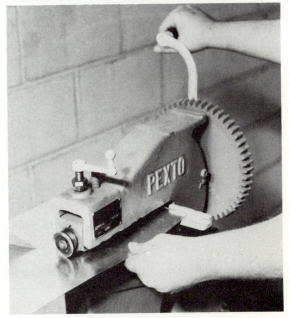

Fig. 3-12 Slitting a sheet

SUMMARY REVIEW

A. Place your answers to the following questions in the column to the right.

1. Name the two types of circle cutting machines.

1. _____
_____

2. Name the parts of a ring and circle shears.

2. _____
_____
_____
_____
_____
_____
_____
_____
_____
_____
_____
_____
_____

3. Why is a ring and circle shears preferred over the circle shears?

3. _____
_____

4. List three types of cutting possible with both machines.

4. _____
_____
_____

5. What range of circle sizes can be cut on the machine in figure 3-2?

_____
_____
_____

B. Insert the correct word or phrase in the following:

1. When cutting light materials, the upper cutting head should be adjusted so that the cutters _____ . _____ but do not rub.

2. The purpose of the clamping discs is to _____ the sheet firmly.

3. When the zero marks on the swivel base line up, the cutting head is set _____ center.

4. The reason for the setting in question 3 is to produce _____ and _____ circles.

C. Underline the correct word or phrase in the following:

1. The slitting gage is used when making (irregular, curved, circle, straight) cuts.

2. The capacity of the ring and circle shears in figure 3-2 is (16, 26, 18, 20) gage.

3. When cutting a heavy metal, the cutters should (touch, rub, be separated slightly).

4. To produce a true circle, the clamped metal must be (off center with, level with, lower than, higher than) the cutters.

5. The slitting gage is used to make straight cuts (perpendicular, parallel, at an angle) to the edge of a sheet.

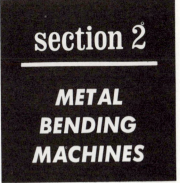

UNIT 4 FOLDER

OBJECTIVES

After studying this unit, the student will be able to

- Name the types of folders used by sheet metal workers.
- List the parts of the bar folder.
- Describe the uses of the bar folder.
- Adjust the bar folder for sheets of various gage sizes.
- Demonstrate the proper procedures for using the bar folders to make hems, folds, and bends.

There are two types of machines used to bend or fold sheet metal to form edges, seams, and angles. A *folder* produces a bend of limited width, while a *brake* produces a bend of unlimited width.

Folders generally are used for folding 22-gage or lighter sheet metal. The various types of folders are bar folders, sheet iron folders, and pipe folders.

Sheet iron folders also are called *cleat benders*. They are used to bend uniform cleat edges up to 30 inches long. The pipe folder is a specialized machine for making locks on formed cylinders

BAR FOLDER

The bar folder consists of a frame, a folding blade, a jaw and fingers (located under the folding blade), and a wing turned by an operating handle, figure 4-1.

When the operating handle is pulled, the jaw under the blade is raised and clamps the sheet between it and the blade. The sheet remains clamped in place while the continued motion of the operating handle completes the bend or fold.

Bar folders are available with working lengths varying from 20 to 42 inches and having a capacity of

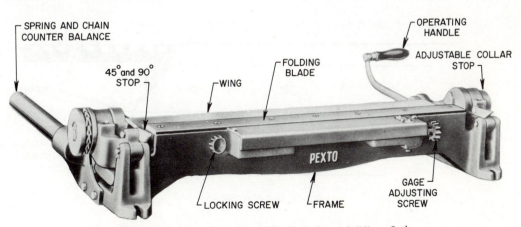

Fig. 4-1 Bar folder (Courtesy of The Peck, Stow, & Wilcox Co.)

Table 4-1

Material	Minimum Fold Width
2X Tin (and lighter)	3/32 inch
No. 24-Gage Mild Steel	1/8 inch
No. 22-Gage Mild Steel	3/16 inch

22 gage for mild steel. The most commonly used working lengths are 20, 30, and 36 inches. Power folders can be obtained if the production of many pieces is required.

Uses

Bar folders are used to bend edges of sheets at various angles, to make channel shapes and double right angle folds, and to prepare folds for lock seams and wired edges. While narrow channel shapes can be formed using a bar folder, reverse bends with small dimensions cannot be formed.

The minimum fold width which can be made on the bar folder depends upon the thickness of the material, see Table 4-1.

The following rules must be observed when using bar folders:

- Material heavier than the rated capacity of the machine must never be folded.

- More than one thickness of material should not be folded, including seams and edges.

- Wire or rod should not be formed in bar folders.

- A hammer or mallet should not be used to flatten sheet metal or straighten wire on the folding blade.

- The bar folder must be kept clean and well-lubricated.

- The wing should be set so as not to bind on the folding blade.

Adjustments

Before using the bar folders, the gage and the wing must be adjusted correctly for the work to be done. The gage adjustment should be checked periodically to insure that the gage markings are correct. The wing must be set to produce the desired sharp or rounded fold. The wing and the distance between the jaw and the folding blade should be adjusted for heavier materials and to prevent the marring of soft materials such as aluminum.

Gage

The width of the fold can be regulated by a gage adjustment screw at the front of the machine.

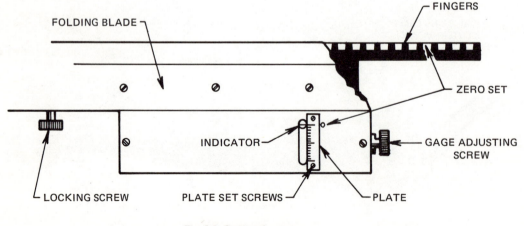

Fig. 4-2 Setting the gage

Fig. 4-3 Setting the wing by loosening the locknut

Fig. 4-4 Wing adjustment

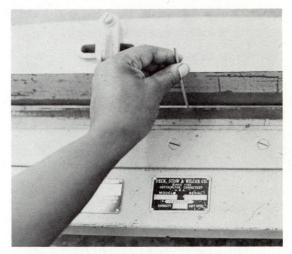

Fig. 4-5 Checking clearance

The gage adjusting screw moves the fingers which act as a stop for the sheet. The gage is usually adjustable from 3/32 inch to 1 inch in 1/16-inch divisions, figure 4-2. The following procedure is used to set the gage.

1. Loosen the locking screw and turn the gage adjusting screw until the fingers are flush with the edge of the folding blade, figure 4-2.

2. The line on the indicator should then be opposite the zero line on the graduated scale; if it is not, loosen the screws and adjust the gage plate.

Wing Adjustment

The sharpness of the fold is regulated by a wedge adjustment, located at the rear of the machine, which lowers or raises the wing, figure 4-3. This adjustment must be made for rounded folds, folds for wired edges, or folding heavy sheets or soft materials such as aluminum.

This adjustment is made by moving the wing back while it is held in a vertical position, figure 4-4. Whenever the wing binds on the folding blade, the wing must be moved to protect the edge.

The following procedure is used to adjust the wing.

1. Raise the wing to a vertical position and hold.

2. Loosen the wedge locknut with a wrench.

3. Move the wedge adjusting screw to the left to lower the blade as far as it will go.

4. Move the wedge adjusting screw to the right until the distance between the wing and the edge of the folding blade is slightly more than the wire diameter or radius of the fold to be made.

5. Check the setting with a piece of wire while the wing is held in a vertical position, figure 4-5.

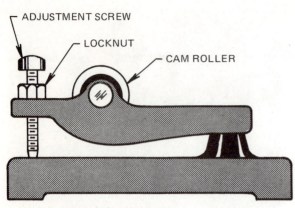

Fig. 4-6 Material thickness adjustment

Fig. 4-7 Stops

6. Tighten the wedge locknut.

7. Return the wing to its original position by lowering the operating handle.

Material Thickness

The clearance between the jaw and the folding blade for various metal thicknesses can be adjusted using the following procedure.

For Heavier Metals

1. Loosen the locknut, figure 4-6.

2. Turn the adjustment screw counterclockwise to lower the cam roller.

3. Place the metal in position and raise the lever. Check the clamping pressure. If the clamps are too tight, continue to adjust as in steps 1 and 2.

For Lighter Metals

1. Proceed as for heavier metals with one exception: turn the adjustment screw clockwise to raise the cam roller.

Collar and Stop Adjustments

45- and 90-Degree Angles

1. Select a stop for 45 or 90 degrees, figure 4-7.

2. Rotate the collar so that the edge lays flat on the frame.

3. Adjust the stops at both ends of the folder.

0- to 180-Degree Angles

1. Make a sheet metal template for the angle desired.

Fig. 4-8 Angle setting with adjustable collar

2. Loosen the clamping bolt on the adjustable collar stop.

3. Place the edge of the template on the folding blade.

4. Rotate the wing until it fits against the template angle.

5. Hold the wing, figure 4-8, and rotate the collar until the stop lays flat on the frame.

6. Tighten the clamping bolt.

BENDS, FOLDS, EDGES

The edges and folds shown in figure 4-9 can be made on a bar folder. To make hems and folds for

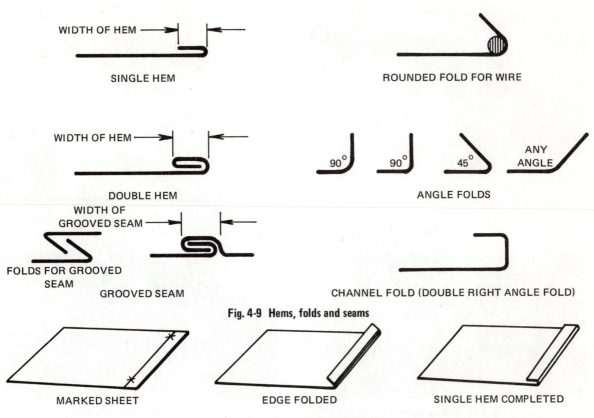

Fig. 4-9 Hems, folds and seams

MARKED SHEET   EDGE FOLDED   SINGLE HEM COMPLETED

Fig. 4-10 Steps for making a single hem

grooved locks, the gage of the bar folder is set slightly less than the width of the hems or the grooved lock.

A.   HOW TO MAKE A SINGLE HEM

The single hem is made in two steps, figure 4-10. First of all, the edge is folded and then it is flattened.

1.   Loosen the locking screw.

2.   With the gage adjusting screw, set the gage slightly less than the width of the hem.

OR:

Place the sheet against the fingers and move the gage until the line marked on the sheet is slightly outside the folding blade.

3.   Tighten the locking screw.

4.   Insert the edge of the metal to be folded between the folding blade and the jaw.

5.   Hold the metal firmly against the gage fingers with the left hand and place the right hand on the operating handle, figure 4-11.

Fig. 4-11 Starting the fold

Fig. 4-12 Making the fold

Fig. 4-13 Flattening the hem

CAUTION   Keep your fingers away from the folding blade.

6. To fold the edge, pull the operating handle
    with the right hand as far as it will go, figure
    4-12. Keep the left hand on the sheet until the
    sheet is held in place by the wing.

7. Return the operating handle to its former posi-
    tion. Keep your hand on the operating handle
    until the wing returns to its normal position.

8. Remove the sheet from the folder and place it
    with the fold facing upward on the beveled part
    of the blade as close as possible to the wing,
    figure 4-13.

9. Pull the operating handle with a swift motion
    to flatten the hem.

B.   HOW TO MAKE A DOUBLE HEM

1. Follow steps 1 to 9 of "How to Make A Single
    Hem," figure 4-14.

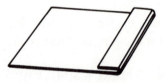

Fig. 4-14 Single hem

Fig. 4-15 Single-hemmed edge folded

Fig. 4-16 Double hem

2. Insert the single-hemmed edge between the jaw
    and the folding blade and repeat operations 4
    to 9 of "How To Make A Single Hem," figures
    4-15 and 4-16.

Note: For light materials, it is not necessary to change the gage setting when making the second fold of the double hem; however, allowances must be made for the thickness of heavy metals.

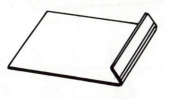

Fig. 4-17 First fold

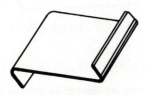

Fig. 4-18 Second fold

SET GAGE TO 1½ x DIA. OF WIRE

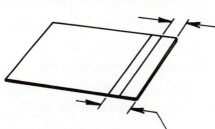

EDGE ALLOWANCE 2½ x DIA. OF WIRE

Fig. 4-19 Layout for wired edge

Fig. 4-20 Fold for wired edge

C. HOW TO MAKE A GROOVED SEAM

1. Set the gage so that it is slightly less than the width of the grooved seam required, or slightly less than the width scribed on the sheet.

2. Insert the edge of the metal to be folded between the folding blade and the jaw.

3. Hold the metal firmly against the gage fingers with the left hand and place the right hand on the operating handle.

4. Pull the operating handle with the right hand as far as it will go to fold the edge, figure 4-17. Keep the left hand on the sheet until the sheet is clamped.

5. Return the operating handle to its former position.

6. Adjust the material so that the other edge to be folded is between the folding blade and the jaw.

7. Make the fold on the second edge, figure 4-18.

D. HOW TO MAKE THE FOLD FOR A WIRE EDGE

1. Set the wing for a rounded fold as in the section on "Wing Adjustment."

2. Set the gage either to 1 1/2 times the diameter of the wire to be used or to the distance scribed on the sheet, figure 4-19.

3. Put the edge of the metal to be folded between the blade and the jaw.

4. Hold the metal firmly against the gage fingers with the left hand and place the right hand on the operating handle.

5. Pull the operating handle as far as possible. Keep your left hand on the sheet until it is clamped.

Fig. 4-21 Angle folds

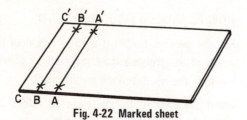
Fig. 4-22 Marked sheet

6. Return the operating handle to its former position and remove the sheet, figure 4-20, page 25. Keep your hand on the operating handle until the wing is back to its normal position.

E. HOW TO MAKE AN ANGLE FOLD

1. Adjust the stop to the desired angle as in the collar and the stop adjustment. Several different round and sharp angle folds are shown in figure 4-21, page 25.

2. Set the gage for the width of the fold required.

3. Insert the sheet between the folding blade and the jaw.

4. Hold the sheet firmly against the gage fingers with your left hand and pull the operating handle as far as possible with your right hand.

5. Hold the formed sheet with your left hand and return the operating handle to its normal position. Remove the sheet.

CAUTION   As with all machine processes, keep your fingers away from the blade. Hold the sheet until it is clamped. Hold the handle until the wing returns to its normal position.

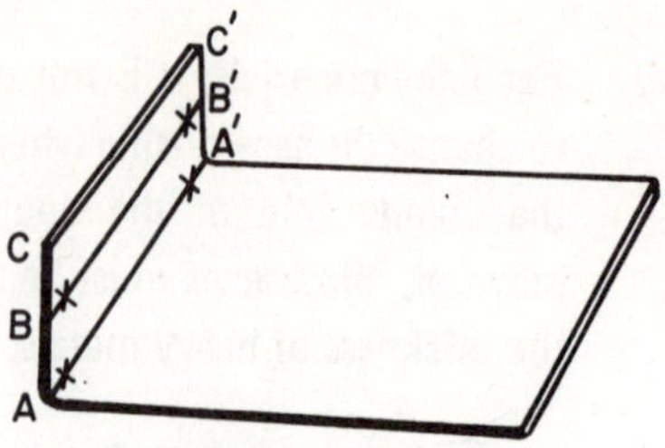

Fig. 4-23 First fold

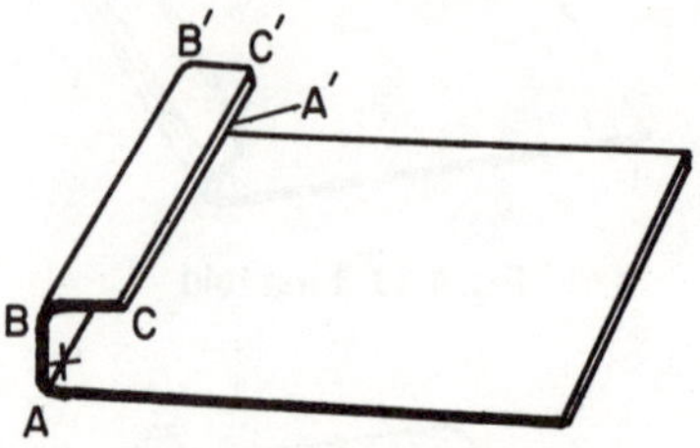

Fig. 4-24 Second fold

F. HOW TO MAKE A DOUBLE ANGLE FOLD

1. Set the gage of the bar folder for the distance C-A or set it to the lines AA', figure 4-22. For a rounded bend, the wing must be moved back as in the section on "Wing Adjustment."

2. Place the 90-degree angle stop in position.

3. Insert the material and make the fold by pulling the operating handle, figure 4-23.

4. Set the gage of the bar folder for distance C-B or set it to the line B B', figure 4-22.

5. Insert the material and make the fold by pulling the operating handle, figure 4-24. If several pieces are required, make all of the A A' folds and then make all of the B B' folds.

SUMMARY REVIEW

A. Place your answers to the following questions in the column to the right.

1. List the three types of folders used in the sheet metal trade.

1. _____

   _____

   _____

2. Name the parts of a bar folder as shown in figure 4-1.

2. _____

   _____

   _____

   _____

   _____

   _____

3. State the three general uses for a bar folder.

3. _____

   _____

   _____

4. Name the three adjustments on a bar folder.

4. _____

   _____

   _____

5. List three steps to take in correcting the gage adjustment on the bar folder.

5. _____

   _____

   _____

6. Name four types of folds that require a wing adjustment on a bar folder.

6. _____

   _____

   _____

   _____

7. List five types of edges and folds that can be made with a bar folder.

7. _____

   _____

   _____

   _____

   _____

B. Insert the correct word or phrase in the following:

1. The minimum width of fold that can be made on a bar folder depends on the _____ of the material.

2. A bar folder should never be used to form _____ or _____ .

3. Sheet metal should not be flattened or straightened on the bar folder with a _____ , or _____ .

4. Never fold more than _____ thickness(es) of metal on the bar folder.

5. When folding metal on a bar folder, always keep your _____ away from the folding blade.

C. Underline the correct word or phrase in the following:

1. The sharpness of the fold is regulated by adjusting the (gage, collar, wing) stops.

2. Folders generally are used for folding (24, 26, 22, 16)-gage sheet metal or lighter.

3. Bar folders are used to bend or fold (wire, rod, band iron, sheet metal).

4. When making hems and folds for grooved locks, the gage of the bar folder is set (equal to, less than, more than) the width of the hem.

5. The maximum working length of a bar folder is (21, 30, 36, 60) inches.

6. The collar and stop adjustment can be set for (any angle, 45 degrees only, 90 degrees only) in making a fold.

UNIT 5 *SLIP ROLL FORMING MACHINE*

OBJECTIVES

After studying this unit, the student will be able to

- List the types of roll forming machines.

- Name the uses of the slip roll forming machine.

- List the parts of the slip roll forming machine.

- Adjust the slip rolls.

- Use the proper procedures to form cylindrical shapes, tapered jobs, and wire-edged jobs.

Roll forming machines are used to form material into curved shapes. There are two general types of roll forming machines commonly used by sheet metal workers. One type has rolls mounted in solid housings while the other type allows one end of the top roll to swing away from the housing. The latter machine is called a *slip roll forming machine.* It is used more often by sheet metal workers because cylinders can be removed from it without distortion.

Special roll forming machines can form many kinds of work, such as pipes with small diameters and special shapes, heavy materials, band iron, and angle iron. Machines can be obtained with special slotted rolls for use in forming flanged-end tank sections, or they can be obtained with rolls for pressing many beads in cylinders.

The maximum thickness of material that roll forming machines can form depends on the diameter and the length of the cylinder to be formed, the stiffness of the sheet, and the uniformity of the diameter required for long cylinders. The capacity of roll forming machines is rated for the full length of soft steel.

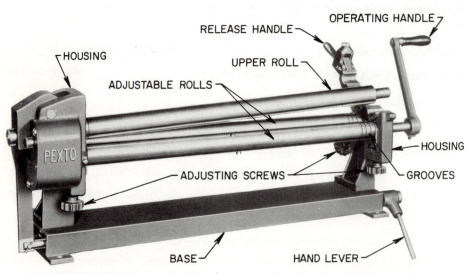

Fig. 5-1 Slip roll forming machine (Courtesy of The Peck, Stow & Wilcox Co.)

SLIP ROLL FORMING MACHINE

A slip roll forming machine consists of a base, two housings, and three rolls. The two front rolls are connected with gears and turned by the operating handle. The gears for the front rolls are enclosed in the left hand housing, figure 5-1.

The two front rolls feed the material while the rear roll deflects the sheet upward to form the curvature. The spacing of the rear roll determines the curvature of the job and is adjusted by knurled adjustment knobs at the rear of each housing. The knurled adjustment knobs on the front of the housings are used to adjust the lower front roll for the thickness of the material, an edge, or a lock.

The bottom front roll and the rear roll have three circular grooves of different radii for rolling jobs with outside wired edges. The grooves can be used to form wire for handles, wired edges, and beaded edges.

One end of the upper roll swings clear of its bearing so that the formed job can be released and removed without distortion. Figures 5-2 and 5-3 show two different types of roll releases. The trigger release shown in figure 5-2 is pulled forward to permit the upper roll to swing toward the operator. The second type of release, figure 5-3, is turned back to permit the upper roll to be raised by the lift handle which automatically locks the roll in a tilted position.

The slip roll forming machine is easy to operate, but experience is required to make well-formed jobs. The distance the rolls should be separated is determined by experimenting with the setting. Tapered jobs are more difficult to roll than cylindrical jobs because of the special technique required.

Slip roll forming machines can roll material varying over a range of thicknesses and widths. Power-driven forming machines also are available. The capacities of the commonly used machines are given in the table at the top of page 30.

Machines with 3-inch diameter rolls, figure 5-4, are furnished with all three rolls driven. The rear roll has three full-length, longitudinal grooves and is operated through a back shaft at a 4:1 gear reduction.

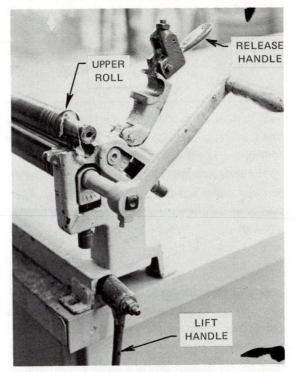

Fig. 5-2 Trigger release

Fig. 5-3 Lift release

Roll Diameter (inches)	Wire Grooves (inch)	Sheet Length (inches)	Gage
2	3/16, 1/4, 5/16	24, 30, 36, 42	20 gage for 24 inch 24 gage for 42 inch
2 1/2	1/4, 9/32, 5/16, 3/8	24, 30, 36, 42	16 gage for 36 inch 20 gage for 42 inch
3	3/8, 1/2, 5/8	24, 30, 36, 42	14 gage for 36 inch 16 gage for 42 inch

Two handles are supplied for the forming of heavy metal. Special materials such as wire mesh can be formed easily on this type of machine.

Highly-polished rolls are available for rolling aluminum, monel metals, and stainless steel. These rolls must be protected when not in use to prevent scratches.

Uses

Slip roll forming machines are used to form jobs with cylindrical shapes such as pipes, stacks, tees and elbows, tanks, ventilators, belt guards, and gear guards as well as tapered cylindrical jobs such as pails, reducers, air scoops, and the heels and throats of square elbows or fittings. Special shapes used in aircraft and ship construction, such as the skin of a fuselage, the leading edge of a wing, and the plates for the hull of a ship, can be formed with slip roll forming machines.

HOW TO ROLL CYLINDRICAL JOBS

1. Raise or lower the bottom front roll by adjusting the two front knurled adjustment knobs. If the sheet has a folded edge, the rolls must be far enough apart so the fold is not flattened.

Note: Wipe off the rolls. When rolling special metals such as aluminum, monel, or stainless steel, the surface of each roll must be clean and free of imperfections so that the material will not be marred.

2. Set the rear roll by adjusting the two knurled screws at the back of the machine. To make a larger diameter, the rear roll must be lowered; to make a smaller diameter, the rear roll must be raised.

Note: There is no set adjustment to produce a certain diameter.

3. Insert the sheet between the rolls from the front of the machine.

Fig. 5-4 Slip roll forming machine with 3-inch diameter rolls

Fig. 5-5 Starting job into rolls

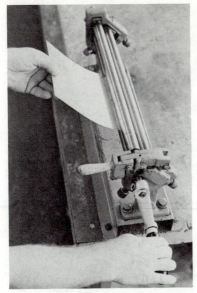  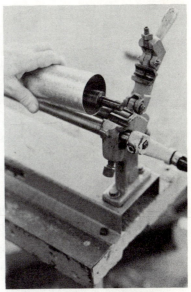

Fig. 5-6 Raising the job to start a curve   **Fig. 5-7 Forming the job**   **Fig. 5-8 Removing finished job**

4. Start the sheet between the rolls by turning the operating handle, figure 5-5.

5. Holding the operating handle firmly with the right hand, raise the sheet with the left hand to form the starting edge, figure 5-6.

   Note: The bend of the edge is determined by the diameter of the job to be formed. If the edge of the job is to be flat, or nearly flat, the edge should not be given a starting bend.

6. Turn the operating handle until the sheet is partially through the rolls, changing the left hand from the front edge of the sheet to the upper edge of the sheet, figure 5-7.

7. Roll the remainder of the sheet through the machine.

   Note: If the curvature of the job is not small enough, bring the sheet back to its starting position by turning the operating handle in the opposite direction, raise the rear roll slightly, and roll the sheet through the rolls. Repeat this procedure until the required curvature is obtained.

   OR

Remove the sheet, raise the rear roll slightly, and roll the sheet through the rolls. Repeat this procedure until the required curvature is obtained.

8. Release the upper roll, figure 5-8, and remove the job.

HOW TO BRAKE TINPLATE

Sharp parallel kinks or wrinkles often appear on jobs made from tinplate. Such wrinkles can be avoided by passing the sheet through the forming rolls several times. The sheet is reversed with each pass and then is straightened by pulling it over the rear roll while making the last pass; this procedure is called *braking tinplate*. Buckling in sheet metal can be removed in the same manner.

HOW TO ROLL A CYLINDRICAL JOB WITH A WIRE EDGE

1. Raise or lower the bottom roll at the front of the machine by adjusting the two front knurled adjustment screws.

   Note: When rolling light-gage material with a wired edge, the distance between the upper and lower roll should be greater at the wired end than at the opposite end.

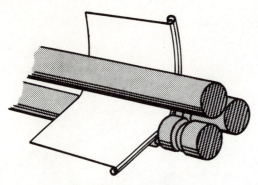

Fig. 5-9 Rolling a wired job

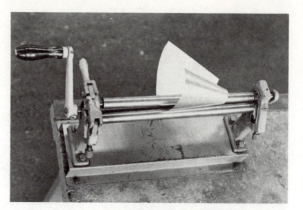

Fig. 5-10 Rolling a tapered job

2. Set the rear roll by adjusting the two knurled screws at the back of the machine.

   Note: When rolling light-gage material with a wired edge, the rear roll should be slightly wider apart at the wired end than at the opposite end.

3. Insert the sheet between the rolls from the front of the machine, placing the wired edge into the proper size groove in the rolls, figure 5-9.

4. Roll the job as in "How To Roll Cylindrical Jobs," steps 4 to 8.

   Note: The wire edge tends to open up if it is rolled excessively.

HOW TO ROLL TAPERING JOBS

1. Raise or lower the front bottom roll so that the sheet can be inserted.

2. Set the rear roll so that the rolls on one end are closer together than on the opposite end, figure 5-10. The exact amount of this adjustment must be found by experimenting with the setting.

3. Insert the sheet between the rolls from the front of the machine.

4. Start the sheet between the rolls by turning the operating handle.

5. Hold the operating handle firmly with the right hand and raise the sheet with the left hand to form a starting edge.

   Note: The bend of the edge is determined by the diameter of the job to be formed.

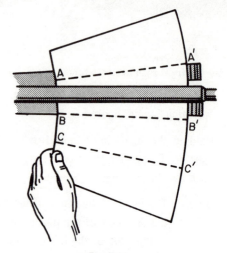

Fig. 5-11

If the edge of the job is to be flat, or nearly flat, the edge should not be given a starting bend.

6. Turn the operating handle with the right hand. Hold the sheet with the left hand at the small end to retard the movement of this end so that the pattern elements AA', BB', and CC' pass the center of the upper roll at the same time, figure 5-11.

   Note: Some machines are equipped with a device which holds the small diameter end of the job while the material is being rolled.

   OR

   Roll the sheet partly through the machine and pull back on the small end until AA' is under the center of the top roll; then continue to roll the sheet and pull it back until BB' is under the rolls. Repeat this until the entire sheet has passed through the rolls.

7. As the material passes through the rolls, hold the left hand on the front edge of the job until the edge is almost through the rolls; then change the left hand from the front edge to the upper edge of the sheet

8. If the curvature is too large or the taper is not correct, readjust the back roll.

9. Reinsert the sheet at the front of the machine and repeat the steps above.

10. Release the upper roll and remove the job.

SUMMARY REVIEW

A. Place your answers to the following questions in the column to the right.

1. Name the two general types of roll forming machines.

   1. _____

     _____

2. List the types of material that can be formed on various roll forming machines.

   2. _____

     _____

     _____

     _____

3. State two uses of the special slotted ends in the rolls.

   3. _____

     _____

4. Name the parts of the slip roll forming machine.

   4. _____

     _____

     _____

     _____

     _____

     _____

     _____

5. List two factors that determine the maximum thickness of material that a roll forming machine can form.

   5. _____

     _____

6. List nine jobs that can be formed on a slip roll forming machine.

   6. _____

     _____

     _____

     _____

     _____

     _____

     _____

     _____

B.   Insert the correct word or phrase in the following:

1.   The two _____ rolls feed the material.

2.   The rear roll _____ the sheet _____ to form the curvature.

3.   The trigger release permits free _____ of the formed job.

4.   When using the slip roll forming machine, keep your _____ and loose _____ away from the rolls.

5.   The grooves can be used to form _____ for handles and _____ edges.

C.   Underline the correct word or phrase in the following:

1.   The slip roll forming machine commonly used by sheet metal workers has a capacity of (16, 20, 22, 24) gage.

2.   Machines with 3-inch diameter rolls or larger enable the operator to roll (lighter, heavier) metal.

3.   A highly-polished roll is used to form (black iron, galvanized iron, aluminum).

4.   The forming of a pipe to a specific diameter is accomplished on a slip roll forming machine by (setting adjustment to that diameter, trial and error).

5.   To form the starting curvature on the edge of a sheet after it is gripped by the front rolls, (lower the sheet, raise the sheet, keep it straight) with the left hand.

UNIT 6 BENDING MACHINES

OBJECTIVES

After studying this unit, the student will be able to

- Name the general types of bending machines.

- List the necessary parts of a bending machine.

- Describe the types of bends that can be made with a bending machine.

- List the material shapes that can be formed on this type of machine.

BENDING MACHINES

The bending of cold metals is a complex process with many technical difficulties resulting from the fact that a physical change occurs within the metal. This change is different with each type of metal and each type of bend.

A variety of *bending machines* is available. The selection of a machine for a sheet metal shop is determined by the range of the bending requirements. Some bending machines are designed for a specific purpose while other machines are designed to handle a variety of materials and bends, figure 6-1.

All bending machines have essentially the same parts: a *form* or *radius collar* which has the same shape as the desired bend, a *clamping block* or *locking pin* that securely grips the material during the bending operation, and a *forming roller* or *follow block* which moves around the bending form.

Bending machines with the following metal bending capacities are available:

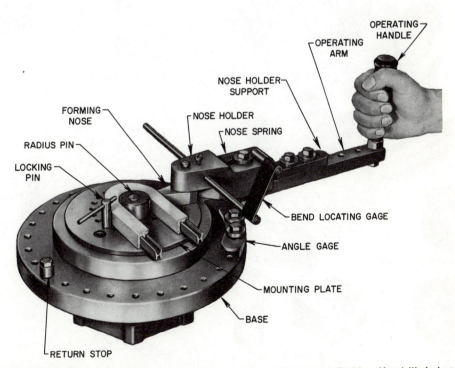

Fig. 6-1 Di-Acro bender All illustrations in this unit are courtesy of The Di-Acro Division, Houdaille Industries, Inc.

1. mild steel rod, 3/16-inch diameter to 1-inch diameter maximum.

2. mild steel bar, 1/8 inch square to 3/4 inch square maximum.

3. steel tubing, 16-gage wall thickness, 5/16-inch diameter to 1 1/4-inch diameter maximum.

4. steel pipe, 1/4-inch I.D. to 1-inch I.D. maximum.

5. flat steel bars bent flat, 1/8 inch x 3/4 inch to 3/8 inch x 4 inch.

6. flat steel bars bent edgewise, 1/16 inch x 1/2 inch to 1/4 inch x 1 inch.

7. angle iron, 1/16 inch x 1/2 inch x 1/2 inch to 3/16 inch x 1 inch x 1 inch.

8. steel channel, 1/16 inch x 1/4 inch x 1/2 inch to 3/16 inch x 1/2 inch x 1 inch.

Bending machines with various forming accessories, figure 6-2, and locking fixtures, figure 6-3, can form a variety of bends on bar, band, rod, or angle steel. Eye bending, zero radius bending, and circle, scroll, square, spring, coil, loop, and spiral bending are several, but not all, of the bends possible using bending machines.

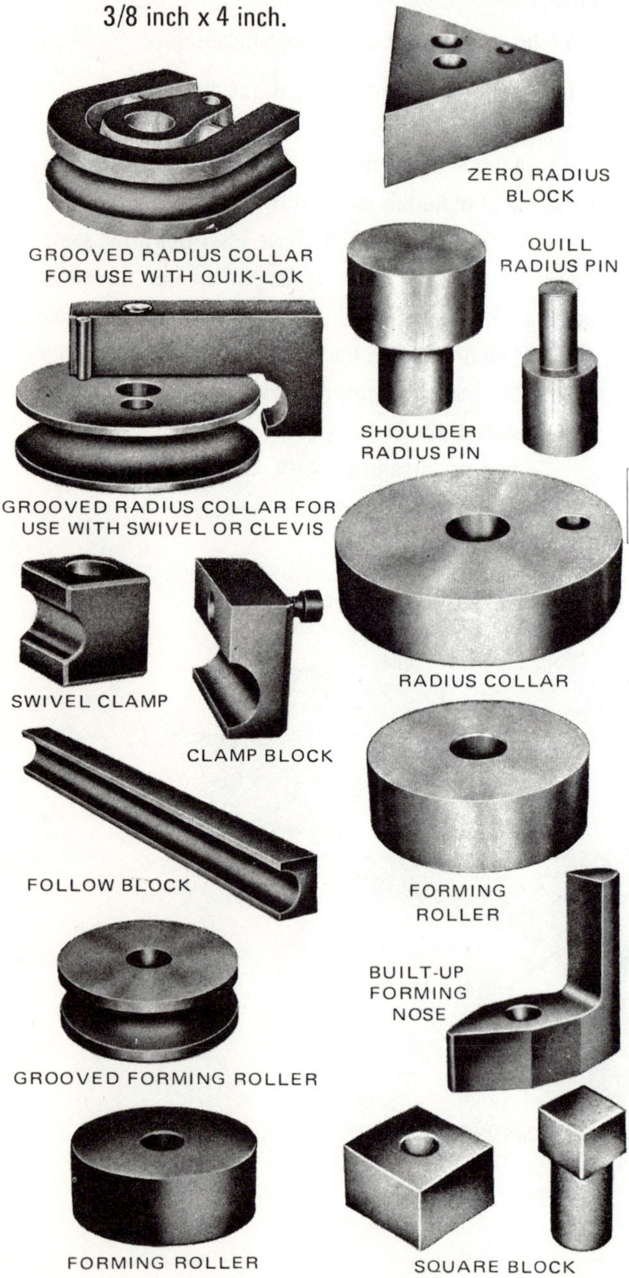

GROOVED RADIUS COLLAR FOR USE WITH QUIK-LOK

ZERO RADIUS BLOCK

GROOVED RADIUS COLLAR FOR USE WITH SWIVEL OR CLEVIS

QUILL RADIUS PIN

SHOULDER RADIUS PIN

STANDARD LOCKING PIN

CLEVIS TUBE CLAMP

SWIVEL CLAMP

CLAMP BLOCK

RADIUS COLLAR

SWIVEL TUBE CLAMP

SPLIT BLOCK TUBE CLAMP

FOLLOW BLOCK

FORMING ROLLER

CAM LOCK FOR LARGE RADII

INSET LOCK PIN

GROOVED FORMING ROLLER

BUILT-UP FORMING NOSE

CAM LOCK FOR SMALL EYES

FORMING ROLLER

SQUARE BLOCK

Fig. 6-2 Forming accessories

Fig. 6-3 Locking fixtures

Since all metals are somewhat elastic, they tend to spring back after they are formed. The amount of springback depends on the type of material being formed, its size and hardness, and the radius of the bend. To allow for springback in bending, select a smaller radius than that required and make an experimental bend to determine the exact finished size.

HOW TO FORM AN OFF-CENTER EYE

1. To reduce the amount of work required and ease the bending effort, install a forming roller, figure 6-4A. The standard forming nose also can be used for this operation.

2. Insert the material between the locking pin and the radius pin and set the forming roller against the material. Lock the material against the radius pin, figure 6-4B. Advance the operating arm until it strikes the angle gage, figure 6-4C.

3. The off-center eye is completed in one operation. Additional parts can be duplicated following the same procedure. The off-center eye is readily formed in all types of solid materials.

HOW TO FORM A CENTERED EYE

1. When the material is too heavy to be formed into a centered eye in one operation, an off-center eye should be made first. The eye then is placed over the locking pin and the centering bend is made around a radius pin of the desired size, figure 6-6A, page 38.

2. It is sometimes possible to form a centered eye in heavy materials in one operation, figure 6-5. The centering bend is obtained by forcing the material against a pin located in a mounting plate hole, figure 6-6B, page 38. If necessary, this pin can be mounted from the bender base.

3. A pipe strap containing three individual bends can be formed in one operation after the eye is formed. In this procedure, the material must be gaged with both ends extending beyond the locking pin so that they can be formed during the centering operation, figure 6-6C, page 38.

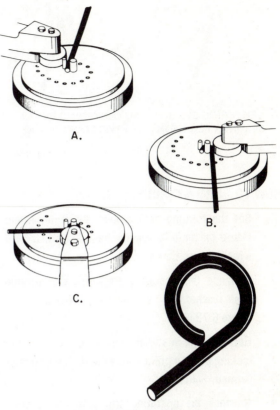

A.

B.

C.

Fig. 6-4 Off-center eye bending

Fig. 6-5 Forming a centered eye

A. CENTERING EYE IN
   SECOND OPERATION

B. CENTERING EYE USING
   TWO LOCKING PINS

C. FORMING PIPE STRAP
   IN ONE OPERATION

Fig. 6-6 Center eye bending

HOW TO FORM A CIRCLE

1. Set the forming nose against the material and clamp the material against the radius collar with a locking pin, figure 6-7A.

2. Advance the operating arm until the forming nose reaches the extreme end of the material, figure 6-7B.

3. Relocate the material and clamp it with the locking pin at a point where the radius is already formed, figure 6-7C.

4. Advance the operating arm until the forming nose again reaches the extreme end of the material, figure 6-7D.

HOW TO FORM A SCROLL

1. Adjust the forming nose so that the material fits snugly between the nose and the high point

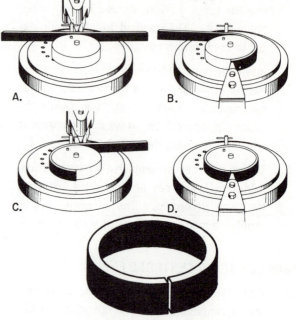

A.

B.

C.

D.

Fig. 6-7 Circle bending

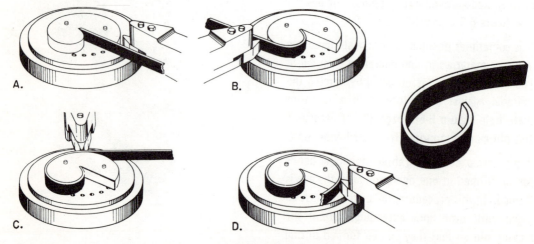

A.

B.

C.

D.

Fig. 6-8 Scroll bending

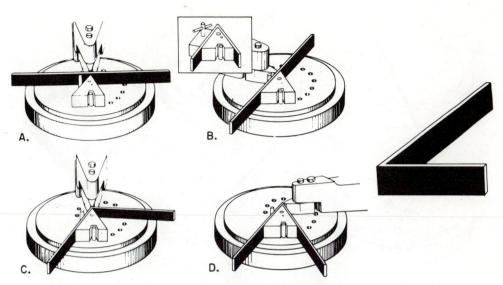

Fig. 6-9 Zero radius bending

of the contour collar; insert the material, figure 6-8A.

2. Advance the operating arm with a steady, even pressure. Note how the material bends only where resistance is offered by the contour collar, figure 6-8B.

3. The material continues to bend and take the shape of the contour collar as the operating arm is advanced, figure 6-8C.

4. As the forming nose reaches the high point of the contour collar, the material is set in the new shape, figure 6-8D.

HOW TO MAKE A ZERO RADIUS BEND

1. Adjust the forming nose so that the material fits snugly between the nose and the apex of the zero radius block, figure 6-9A.

2. Clamp the material close to the bending edge using the locking pin or the holding block, figure 6-9B.

3. Advance the operating arm until it strikes the angle gage to establish the exact degree of the bend, figure 6-9C.

4. Complete the bend, figure 6-9D. Additional parts may be duplicated by repeating the operation.

HOW TO MAKE A SQUARE BEND

1. Adjust the forming nose so that the material fits snugly between the nose and any edge of a square block, figure 6-10A, page 40.

2. Clamp the material between the locking pin and the square block and then advance the operating arm, figure 6-10B, page 40.

3. Note how the material remains straight between the corners of the block as the forming nose moves into position for the second bend, figure 6-10C, page 40.

4. Figure 6-10D, page 40, shows that two bends are complete. It will be necessary to allow additional material if a third bend is required. Advance the operating arm to make a third bend.

HOW TO BEND CHANNEL

Flange In

1. Insert the material in the slots in the radius collar and position the follow block between the channel and the forming roller; tighten the center bolt, figure 6-11A, page 40.

2. Clamp the channel tightly. Advance the operating arm with a steady, even pressure until it strikes a stop preset for the angle of the bend, figure 6-11B, page 40.

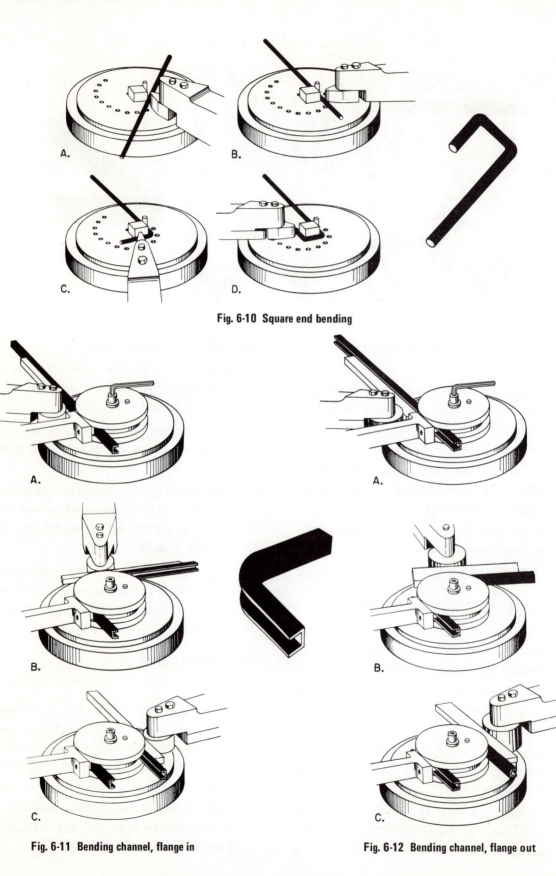

Fig. 6-10 Square end bending

Fig. 6-11 Bending channel, flange in

Fig. 6-12 Bending channel, flange out

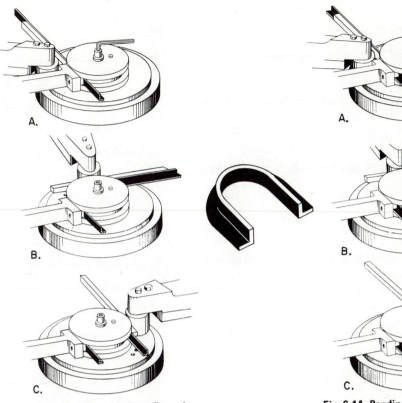

Fig. 6-13 Bending angle iron, flange in

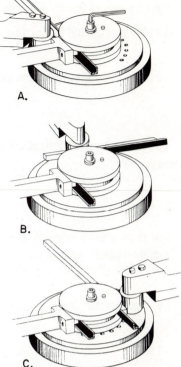

Fig. 6-14 Bending angle iron, flange out

3. Loosen the center bolt, release the clamp, remove the follow block, and slide the material out of the radius collar, figure 6-11C.

Flange Out

1. Position the material in the slots in the radius collar. Insert the follow block in the channel and tighten the center bolt as shown in figure 6-12A.

2. Clamp the channel tightly. Advance the operating arm with a steady, even pressure until it strikes a stop preset for the angle of the bend, figure 6-12B.

3. Loosen the center bolt, release the clamp, remove the follow block, and slide the material out of the radius collar, figure 6-12C.

HOW TO BEND ANGLE IRON

Flange In

1. Insert the material in the slot in the radius collar, position the follow block between the angle and

the forming roller, and tighten the center bolt, figure 6-13A.

2. Clamp the angle tightly. Advance the operating arm with a steady, even pressure until it strikes the angle stop, figure 6-13B.

3. Loosen the center bolt, release the clamp, remove the follow block, and slide the material out of the radius collar, figure 6-13C.

Flange Out

1. Position the material in the radius collar, insert the follow block, and tighten the center bolt, figure 6-14A.

2. Clamp the angle tightly. Advance the operating arm with a steady, even pressure until it strikes the angle stop, figure 6-14B.

3. Loosen the center bolt, release the clamp, remove the follow block, and slide the material out of the radius collar, figure 6-14C.

SUMMARY REVIEW

A.   Place your answers to the following questions in the column to the right.

1.   List the two general types of bending machines.

1.   _____

_____

2.   List the three essential parts of any bending machine.

2.   _____

_____

_____

3.   List four causes of springback in metals that are being bent.

3.   _____

_____

_____

_____

4.   List three general types of bends that can be made with a modern bending machine.

4.   _____

_____

_____

5.   List four metal stock shapes that can be bent in a bending machine.

5.   _____

_____

_____

_____

B.   Insert the correct word or phrase in the following:

1.   Bending involves a _____ change within the metal.

2.   All metals are somewhat _____ .

3.   To allow for springback, a form with a(an) _____ radius than that required is selected.

4.   The capacity of a bending machine for mild steel rod is _____ .

5.   The purpose of a clamping block is to _____ the material during the bending operation.

C.   Underline the correct word or phrase in the following:

1.   The bending machine is capable of bending a (1, 1 1/2, 1/2)-inch square, mild steel bar.

2.   A bending machine is used to form a(an) (hem, flange, off-center eye).

3.   Stainless steel band has (more, less, equal) springback than aluminum.

4.   An angle iron flange collar can be made with a (bar folder, beading machine, bending machine).

5.   A (3/8, 1 1/4, 1 1/2)-inch inside diameter steel pipe can be bent to form a circle in a bending machine.

UNIT 7 STANDARD HAND BRAKES

OBJECTIVES

After studying this unit, the student will be able to

- List the types of hand brakes used by sheet metal workers.

- State the purpose of a hand brake.

- List the necessary safety precautions when operating a hand brake.

- List the major parts of a standard hand brake.

Several types of machines are used by the sheet metal worker to bend, form, or fold sheet metal. The most common of these machines is the *brake.* Several types of brakes include the *standard, hand, box-and pan, universal,* and *letter forming* brakes. Both stationary and portable models are available with hand- or power-operated features. The standard hand brake is commonly found in sheet metal shops. The brake differs from the folder in that the brake is unlimited in the width of the edge that it can form.

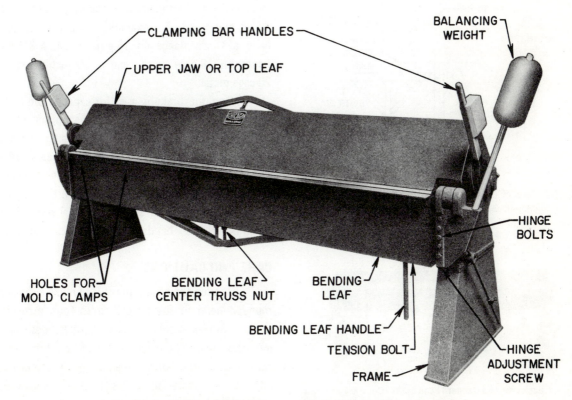

CLAMPING BAR HANDLES

BALANCING WEIGHT

UPPER JAW OR TOP LEAF

HINGE BOLTS

HOLES FOR MOLD CLAMPS

BENDING LEAF CENTER TRUSS NUT

BENDING LEAF

BENDING LEAF HANDLE

TENSION BOLT

FRAME

HINGE ADJUSTMENT SCREW

Fig. 7-1 **Standard hand brake** (Courtesy of Dreis & Krump Manufacturing Co.)

HAND BRAKES

There are two general types of standard hand brakes: the Chicago and the Whitney-Jensen. Both brakes are operated in a similar manner but the adjustments differ slightly. The descriptions and procedures that follow are for a Chicago Standard Hand Brake made by the Dreis & Krump Manufacturing Company.

The Chicago Standard Hand Brake, figure 7-1, page 43, has many advantages over brakes of earlier designs, many of which are still in operation. These advantages include an all-welded, rugged body construction, quick and positive adjustments, and easy operation.

Parts

The standard hand brake consists of a welded steel frame with an attached upper jaw (top leaf) moved by two clamping bar handles, and a lower

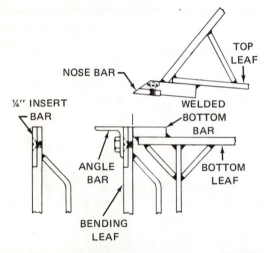

Fig. 7-2 Parts of the standard hand brake (Courtesy of Dreis & Krump Manufacturing Co.)

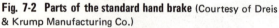
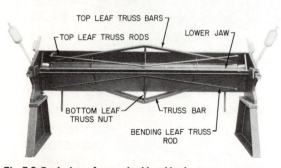

Fig. 7-3 Back view of a standard hand brake (Courtesy of Dreis & Krump Manufacturing Co.)

bottom leaf, figure 7-2. The metal is formed by a bending leaf which is moved by bending leaf handles. Two balancing bars with adjustable weights are attached to the bending leaf to make braking easier. The top, bottom, and bending leaves are braced by truss rods and bars which can be adjusted to insure that the brake will bend the sheet evenly, figure 7-3.

The bending leaf is recessed to receive a 1/4-inch wide steel insert bar; this bar is removable for making narrow, reverse bends, figure 7-2. An angle bar is provided with the brake and is used when braking heavy-gage and long sheet metal pieces.

Capacity

Standard hand brakes are available in bending lengths of 48 1/2, 73, 97, 121, and 145 inches. The capacity of these machines in material thickness ranges from 12-gage mild steel and 16-gage stainless steel, to 22-gage mild steel and 26-gage stainless steel.

All brakes are rated for a 1-inch flange or wider on mild steel. Flanges narrower than 1 inch can be formed on lighter metal. For each 1/4-inch reduction in flange size, the thickness of the metal must be reduced two gages. For example, a machine is rated to bend a 1-inch flange on 16-gage metal, a 3/4-inch flange on 18-gage metal, and a 1/2-inch flange on 20-gage metal.

When the brake is used for capacity work, the reinforcing angle bar must be in the normal or top position, figure 7-2. When the angle bar is removed, the capacity of the brake is reduced four gages. When the 1/4-inch insert bar is removed, reducing the bending leaf edge to a thickness of 1/4-inch, the capacity of the machine is reduced an additional seven gages. Minimum reverse bends of 1/4 inch can be made.

CARE AND CAUTIONS

The purpose of any brake is to make a sharp or rounded bend in sheet metal or to form a specific shape. Brakes should be used for these designated purposes only. The machine should be lubricated at least once a week with a medium grade of machine oil, such as Number 30. Holes for oiling are provided on the moving parts of the machine. Sliding parts that are adjusted infrequently should be lubricated less often than the other moving parts.

To use the brake properly, follow the precautions listed below.

- Bend short pieces of material in the center of the brake to equalize the strain on the machine.

- Never bend against any seams unless the links are adjusted to clamp the full multiple thickness of the seam and the top leaf is set back to clear the same full multiple thickness.

- Always have both the angle bar and the insert bar mounted on the bending leaf when bends are to be made at the full capacity of the machine.

- When forming wide sections, such as cornices, start the bend near the center of sheet to equalize the buckling or wrinkling of the sheet. An alternative method is to make a kink in the opposite end of the sheet from the initial bend.

- Sheets are not always perfectly flat. A buckle left in one end while the other is straightened by clamping in the brake will throw the first bend out of line when it, in turn, is straightened.

- Always use material with sheared square edges; do not use rolled edges as these cause the material to bow.

- Never use a brake to bend rods, wire, or band iron as these materials will damage the nose bar.

- Always adjust the brake for differences in gages. Never use pipe extensions on the clamp handles to gain extra leverage to force-clamp the top on material heavier than that for which the links and top are set.

- Never exceed the rated capacity of the brake.

- Never hammer on the brake.

SAFETY

When using the hand-operated brake, the sheet metal worker must always:

1. Keep his fingers away from the clamping bar and the bending leaf.

2. Keep clear of the bending leaf handles.

3. Be sure that his helper's fingers are clear of the clamping bar and the balancing weights.

4. Be sure that his helper is clear of the bending leaf handle before he raises it.

ADJUSTMENTS

Bending Edge Alignment

When the bending leaf is in the down position, the edge of the leaf should be flush with the edge of the bottom bar.

To adjust the bending leaf to maintain this alignment, first use a level to insure that the brake is level on the floor. If the brake is not level, then

1. Adjust the center of the bending leaf with the truss nut.

2. Adjust the bottom center with a truss nut.

3. Adjust the bending leaf ends with the hinge adjustment screws.

4. Loosen the hinge bolts before making any adjustments and then tighten them after making the above adjustments.

Bowed Bending Leaf Adjustment

If the bending leaf becomes bowed in the center after use, tighten both tension bolts until the center is again a straight line.

Adjusting for Metal Thickness

The clearance for bends is obtained by moving the top leaf back at the bending edge. If the material to be bent is within four gage thicknesses of the capacity of the machine, move the top leaf back a distance equal to twice the thickness of the material. When a lighter material is used, move the top leaf a proportional distance. If sharper bends are desired:

1. Unclamp the handles slightly.

2. Adjust the top leaf with the top adjustment handles.

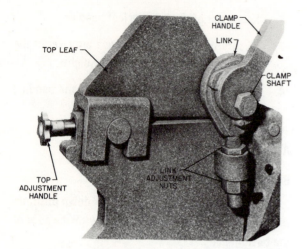

Fig. 7-4 Front-to-back adjustment for material of various gages (Courtesy of Dreis & Krump Manufacturing Co.)

Fig. 7-5 Adjusting the brake clamping pressure with a crescent wrench (Courtesy of Dreis & Krump Manufacturing Co.)

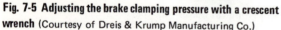
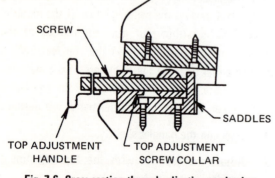

Fig. 7-6 Cross section through adjusting mechanism

The clamping pressure of the links is changed by adjusting the nuts, figures 7-4 and 7-5.

Counterbalance

The counterweight can be raised or lowered on the rod to counterbalance the bending leaf.

Overbending Adjustment

If the sheet bends over more on one side than on the other, set the top leaf back on the end where the sheet is overbending.

1. Unclamp the handle slightly on the side that is overbending.

2. Adjust the top leaf with the top adjustment handle.

3. Reclamp the handle.

Creeping Top Leaf Adjustments

If the top leaf creeps forward when clamping the material:

1. Check that the brake is level on the floor.

2. Insure that the top adjustment screw collars are locked into position so that the screws cannot move back and forth in the saddles. The front shoulder of the screws and the face of the collars must be snug against the saddles with minimal clearance, figure 7-6.

3. If the top leaf still creeps, place a wedge under the rear of the leg at the end that is creeping; increase the height of the wedge until the top leaf stops creeping. Replace the wedge with a permanent block of the correct height.

HOW TO MAKE SHARP BENDS ON THIN METAL

1. Open the right-hand clamping bar by pushing back on the clamping bar handle with the right hand. For a long sheet, open both of the clamping bar handles.

2. Insert the sheet between the upper and lower jaws from the front of the machine. Mark the bend line with a prick punch.

Fig. 7-7 Clamping the left side of the sheet

Fig. 7-8 Clamping the right side of the sheet

3. Place the sheet with the center of the prick punch mark on the left side of the sheet flush with the edge of the clamping bar. Hold the sheet in place with the left hand and pull the clamping bar handle with the right hand until the left side of the sheet is held firmly, figure 7-7.

4. Place the left hand on the right side of the sheet and move the sheet until the center of the prick punch mark on the right side is flush with the clamping bar.

5. Finish clamping the sheet in place by pulling the clamping bar handle with the right hand as far as possible, figure 7-8.

6. Place the right hand on the balancing weight arm and the left hand on the bending leaf handle, figure 7-9.

7. Raise the bending leaf to the desired position for the bend required. It may be necessary to raise the bending leaf a few degrees more than the required angle to allow for the metal to spring back.

8. Gradually return the bending leaf, keeping your hand on the bending leaf handle until it is back to its original position.

9. Open the clamping bars and remove the sheet.

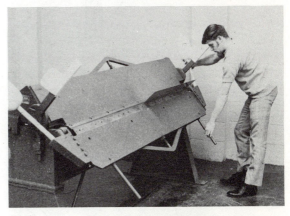

Fig. 7-9 Making the bend

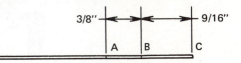

Fig. 7-10 Bend marks

HOW TO FORM THE POCKET FOR A PITTSBURGH LOCK

Layout and prick mark the progressive bends, figure 7-10. Refer to figure 7-11, page 48, for each step of the procedure.

Step 1

1. Insert the sheet in the brake to prick mark A.

2. Close the upper jaw flush to mark A.

3. Raise the bending leaf until the sheet forms slightly less than a 90-degree angle.

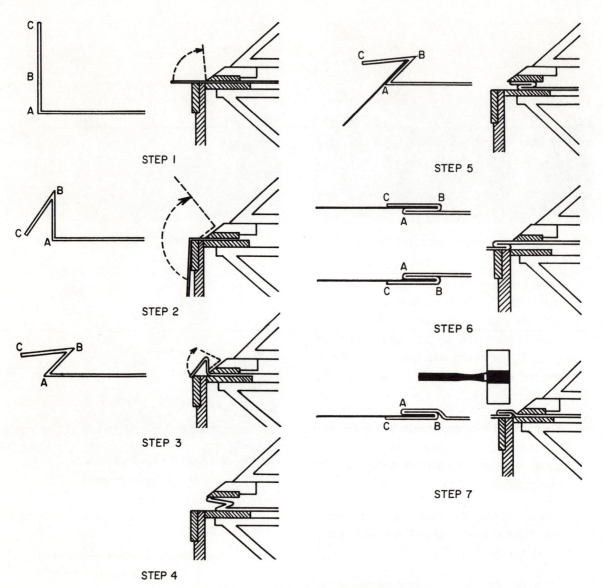

STEP 1

STEP 2

STEP 3

STEP 4

STEP 5

STEP 6

STEP 7

Fig. 7-11 Forming the pocket for a Pittsburgh lock

Step 2

1. Insert the formed edge in the brake.
2. Hold the sheet against the bending leaf.
3. Close the upper jaw.
4. Raise the bending leaf as far as possible.

Step 3

1. Insert the sheet in the brake so that the 90-degree bend is against the edge of the upper jaw.
2. Hold the sheet in this position.
3. Close the upper jaw.
4. Raise the bending leaf as far as possible.

Fig. 7-12 Hand brake with standard formers in 5/8-, 1-, 1 5/8-, 2 1/4-, and 3-inch sizes. (Courtesy of Dreis & Krump Manufacturing Co.)

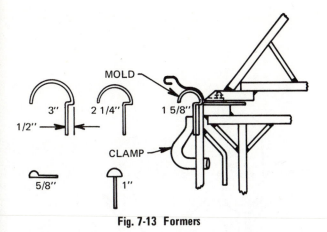

Fig. 7-13 Formers

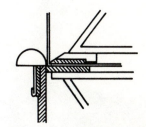
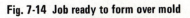

Fig. 7-14 Job ready to form over mold

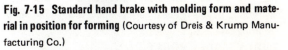

Fig. 7-15 **Standard hand brake with molding form and material in position for forming** (Courtesy of Dreis & Krump Manufacturing Co.)

Step 4

1. Insert the sheet in the brake with the upper edge flush against the outer edge of the upper jaw.

Step 5

1. Insert a piece of scrap metal to maintain the clearance.

2. Close the upper jaw.

Step 6

1. Turn the sheet over.

2. Insert the sheet in the brake with the outer bent edge flush with the outer edge of the bending leaf.

3. Close the upper jaw.

Step 7

1. Raise the bending leaf slightly.

2. Offset the pocket by striking the outer edge with a mallet.

3. Remove the piece of scrap metal.

MOLDS OR FORMERS

When forming curved shapes, *molds* are used on the brake. The standard hand brake is furnished with a set of five mold formers, figure 7-12. Each mold can be clamped in place on the brake with friction clamps.

HOW TO ATTACH FORMERS

1. Place the 1/2-inch clearance side provided on each former against the bending leaf, figure 7-13.

2. Position the clamps and tap them lightly with a mallet. This creates enough friction to hold the forming mold in place.

3. To remove the friction clamps, tap upward on them or turn them.

HOW TO USE FORMERS

Although sharp and rounded angles are made by the brake, curved shapes must be made over the forming molds by hand.

1. Bend the job to be formed to a right angle.

2. Fasten the mold to the brake.

3. Insert the job in the brake and close both clamping bar handles, figure 7-14.

4. Place both hands on the job, figure 7-15.

5. Bend the job over the mold as far as necessary, figure 7-16, page 50.

6. Release the clamping bar handles and remove the job.

Fig. 7-16 Standard hand brake with material bent over molding form to desired radius (Courtesy of Dreis & Krump Manufacturing Co.)

EARLY MODEL BRAKE

Many sheet metal shops still use an early model of the standard hand brake. It is important, therefore, that the sheet metal worker be able to adjust this type of brake as well as the modern model. The adjustments for the bending edge alignment and the bowed bending leaf are the same for both models. Other adjustments are as follows:

Metal Bending Adjustment

1. Cut a small sample of the metal to be formed.

2. Referring to figure 7-17, loosen cap screw (O) with an adjustable wrench.

3. Move the bending leaf into the horizontal position.

4. Adjust setscrews (M) and (P) until the sample fits snugly between the edges of the bending leaf and the top leaf.

5. Tighten setscrew (O).

Metal Clamping Pressure

1. Loosen setscrews (BB) and (FF), figure 7-17.

2. Place the metal sample between the top leaf and the lower jaw.

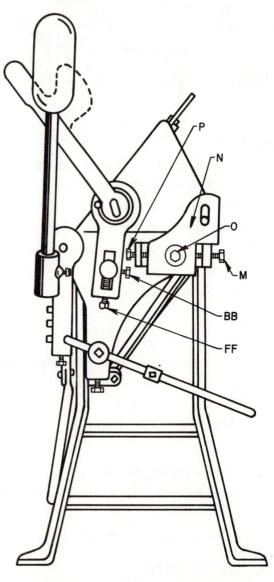

Fig. 7-17 An early model of a brake

3. Bring the top leaf down to rest on the sample. The force on the sample should be the weight of the top leaf only.

4. Adjust setscrew (FF) until link block (EE) is held in the existing position.

5. Tighten setscrew (BB).

SUMMARY REVIEW

A. Place your answers to the following questions in the column to the right.

1. List four types of brakes used in the sheet metal trade.

1. _____
_____
_____
_____

2. Name three general forming operations that can be accomplished with a brake.

2. _____
_____
_____

3. State three types of steel forms that should not be formed on the brake.

3. _____
_____
_____

4. List two general safety precautions a brake operator should observe.

4. _____
_____

5. List the major parts of a standard hand brake.

5. _____
_____
_____
_____
_____
_____

6. State three advantages of the modern standard hand brake.

6. _____
_____
_____

7. What are the adjustments that can be made on the standard hand brake?

7. _____
_____
_____
_____

B. Insert the correct word or phrase in the following:

1. The brake differs from the folder in that the _____ of the edge that can be formed is _____ .

2. Never _____ on a brake.

3. Always place the piece to be formed so that the _____ is equalized throughout the brake.

4. The two general types of standard hand brakes are the _____ and the _____ .

5. When braking heavy gage sheet or long pieces, a(an) _____ is used on the bending leaf.

6. To maintain bending edge alignment, make sure the brake is _____ on the floor.

7. If the bending leaf becomes bowed in the center after use, tighten both of the _____ until the center is brought into a straight line.

C. Underline the correct word or phrase in the following:

1. Clearance for bends is obtained by moving the (bending leaf, top leaf) back at the bending edge.

2. Bend short pieces of metal at the (end, center) of the brake to equalize the strain.

3. Only (rod, wire, seams, bands, flat sheets) should be bent on the brake.

4. The standard hand brake can be used to form the pocket of a (snap lock, riveted lap, Pittsburgh lock).

5. After completing a bend, the bending leaf on the hand brake is (released quickly, returned gradually).

6. The bending leaf is usually raised a few degrees (more than, less than, equal to) the required angle to allow for springback.

7. The purpose of molds or formers on a hand brake is to permit the bending of (right angles, oblique angles, curves).

8. Molds are attached to the (upper jaw, lower jaw, bending leaf) on a hand brake.

UNIT 8 *BOX-AND-PAN BRAKE — UNIVERSAL BRAKE*

OBJECTIVES

After studying this unit, the student will be able to

- List the major parts of the box-and-pan brake and the universal brake.
- State the advantages of the box-and-pan brake and the universal brake.
- List the types of bends that can be made on each of the brakes.
- Select the proper fingers and attachments to be used for a particular job.
- Demonstrate the proper methods of using the box-and-pan brake and the universal brake.

BOX-AND-PAN BRAKE

The *box-and-pan brake*, figure 8-1, is essentially a standard hand brake with all of the features of a standard hand brake. Rather than the solid nose bar, however, the box-and-pan brake has removable sectioned fingers which offer added depth, increased clearance, and a greater range of uses in the sheet metal shop, figure 8-2, page 54.

This type of brake is used to form an object, such as a box or pan with four sides and a bottom and a narrow return flange on the top of a box, from one sheet of metal.

The box-and-pan brake is used to form electrical and electronic switch boxes, cutout boxes, panelboard cabinets, tote boxes, conveyor buckets, and television and radio chassis.

Capacity

The box-and-pan brake is rated to form a 1-inch flange or wider on mild steel. This is the same rating as for the standard hand brake. Narrower flanges can be bent on lighter metal. The reinforcing angle bar must be in its normal position to do work at the capacity of the brake.

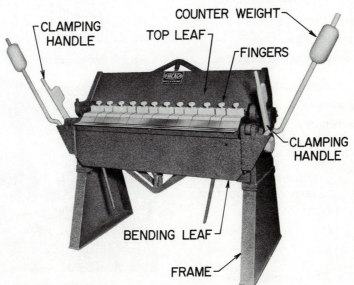

Fig. 8-1 Box-and-pan brake (Courtesy of Dreis & Krump Manufacturing Co.)

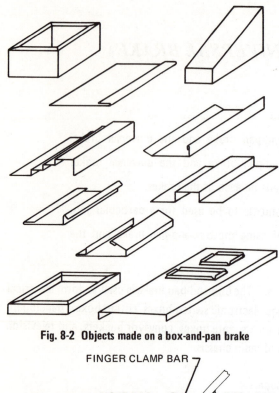

Fig. 8-2 Objects made on a box-and-pan brake

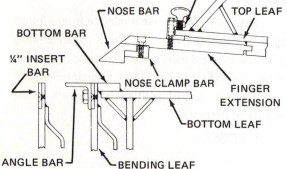

Fig. 8-3 Box-and-pan brake — standard construction

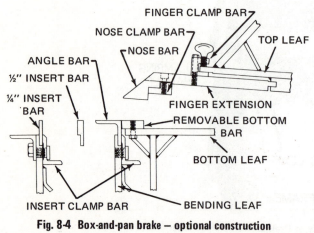

Fig. 8-4 Box-and-pan brake — optional construction

Fingers

Fingers are made of rolled steel bars to provide maximum strength and light weight. They are adjusted or removed by loosening and tightening the thumbscrew. A standard assortment of fingers includes several bars each of widths of 3, 4, 5, and 6 inches. By grouping the fingers, any length can be obtained from 3 inches to the full length of the machine.

Brakes are available either in the standard construction, figure 8-3, or the optional construction, figure 8-4. The bottom bar is stationary on the standard model brake and it is removable on the optional model brake. The removable bottom bar feature means that the bending edge can be renewed whenever required.

Nose Bars

The *nose bar* is interchangeable so that special bars such as the radius bars shown in figures 8-5 and 8-6 can be used to make radius bends, figure 8-7. Radius nose sizes from 1/32 inch to 1 1/2 inches are available, as are full-length radius nose bars.

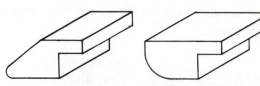

Fig. 8-5 Radius nose bar   **Fig. 8-6 Radius nose bar**

Fig. 8-7 Radius nose bar used instead of straight bending fingers for forming contemporary furniture

(Figures 8-3 to 8-7, Courtesy of Dreis & Krump Manufacturing Co.)

Fig. 8-8   Bridge-type nose bar extended between fingers to form tubular shapes

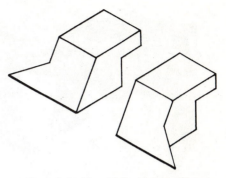

Fig. 8-9   Right and left extension fingers

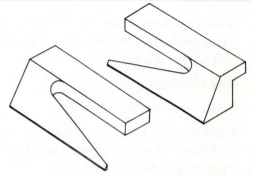

Fig. 8-10   Right and left open-end fingers

Tubular shapes can be formed by extending bridge-type nose bars between the fingers, figure 8-8. With the fingers placed in their normal positions, large tubular shapes can be formed by allowing the metal to spring out of shape against the top side of the fingers. In most metals the shape is distorted only while it is being finished. As soon as the tube is removed from the brake, the metal springs back to the correct shape. Deep channels can be formed using finger extensions.

Right and left extension fingers, figure 8-9, are used to form the inside corners of boxes, cabinets, or chassis with a return flange across the top.

Open-end fingers, figure 8-10, are used to form triangular, square, tapered, and rectangular tubes. The formed part easily slips off the open end of the finger.

ADJUSTMENTS

The adjustments described for the standard hand brake also apply to the box-and-pan brake. These adjustments include metal thickness, bend allowance, bending edge alignment, leaf bow bending, and top leaf creeping.

HOW TO FORM A BOX

1. Lay out the box on a flat sheet to the given dimensions.

2. Cut out the desired shape, figure 8-11.

3. Select a group of fingers equal to the distance from bend line 1 to bend line 3.

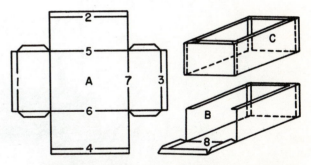

Fig. 8-11 Sequence of operations in forming a box shape with inside flanges (Figures 8-8 to 8-10 courtesy of Dreis & Krump Manufacturing Co.)

4. Set the fingers in place on the top leaf.

5. Adjust the brake for the metal thickness and the bend allowance.

6. Place the sheet in the brake to bend line 1 and close the top leaf.

7. Make a 90-degree bend at line 1.

8. Repeat steps 6 and 7 to make bends at lines 2, 3, and 4.

Fig. 8-12 Operator making the final bend in a typical pan forming operation.

9. Replace the sheet in the brake at line 5. The fingers should cover the full width of the sheet from line 1 to line 3.

10. Make a 90-degree bend.

11. Repeat steps 9 and 10 on bend line 6.

12. Adjust the finger width to fit the length of line 7. Remove the excess fingers on both ends as shown in figure 8-12.

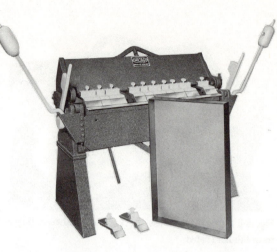

Fig. 8-13 A completed box shaped on the box-and-pan brake

13. Place the sheet in the brake up to bend line 7. The fingers must fit inside the tabs.

14. Make a 90-degree bend.

15. Place the last side in the brake up to bend line 8.

16. Close the top leaf.

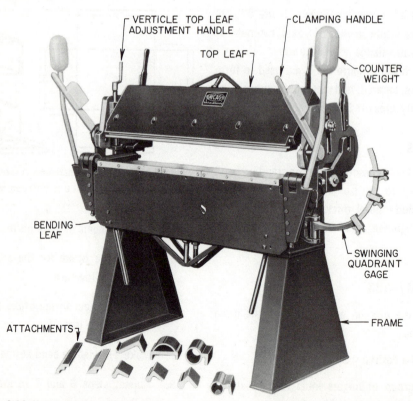

VERTICLE TOP LEAF ADJUSTMENT HANDLE

CLAMPING HANDLE

TOP LEAF

COUNTER WEIGHT

BENDING LEAF

SWINGING QUADRANT GAGE

ATTACHMENTS

FRAME

Fig. 8-14 Universal brake (Figures 8-12 to 8-14 courtesy of Dreis & Krump Manufacturing Co.)

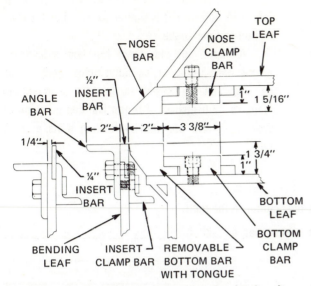

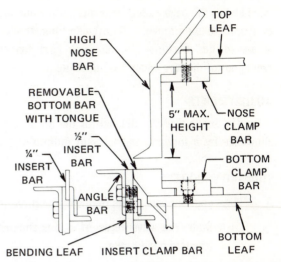

Fig. 8-15   Cross section of a universal brake showing the method of holding all bending edges securely.

Fig. 8-16   Cross section of a universal high top combination brake

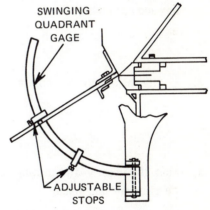

Fig. 8-17   Cross section of a swinging quadrant gage with adjustable stops

17. Raise the bending leaf to make a 90-degree bend.

18. Open the top leaf and remove the finished box, figure 8-13.

UNIVERSAL BRAKE

The *universal hand brake*, figure 8-14, makes all of the various types of bends used in sheet metal work. This type of brake has all of the essential and desirable features of other hand brake models.

The universal hand brake has a capacity of 14-gage mild steel or 18-gage stainless steel and is available with bending lengths of 48, 72, 96, and 120 inches.

Attachments

The cross section of the universal brake, figure 8-15, shows a sharp nose bar used in combination with a removable bottom bar and an insert bar to provide a means of forming internal flanges and irregular flanges. Nose bars, bottom bars, and insert bars are available in any length. The proper use of these attachments allows the sheet metal worker to bend internal flanges or flanges on only one part of a sheet while leaving the remainder of the sheet flat.

The cross section in figure 8-16 shows a high nose bar attachment clamped in place with a nose

clamp bar. These 90-degree bars made from Z sections are available in any length from 1 to 120 inches. They are used to form one-piece boxes up to 5 inches deep.

Other attachments for the universal brake are low radius nose bars with a 1 1/2-inch maximum radius and high radius nose bars with 1 1/2-, 2 1/2-, or 3 1/2-inch maximum radii. The standard angle bar is used on the 1 1/2-inch radius bars while a bumper bar and a special angle bar are used on bars with radii of 2 1/2 inches and larger.

Gage

Each universal brake is equipped on one end with a *swinging quadrant gage* with adjustable stops, figure 8-17, page 57. Any angle of bend can be maintained when this gage is used, regardless of the number of pieces to be formed. To provide unobstructed access to the machine, the quadrant gage can be swung out of the way when it is not in use.

ADJUSTMENTS

The brake itself is adjusted for the metal bend allowance by a forward or backward motion of the top leaf about an eccentric pin at each end of the leaf. This adjustment is similar to the adjustment on the box-and-pan brake.

A rapid up and down top leaf adjustment can be made using vertical adjustment screws. The top leaf can be raised to provide a maximum clearance of 5 inches. The top leaf can be clamped securely in any position by locking bolts at each end.

SUMMARY REVIEW

A.   Place your answers to the following questions in the column to the right.

1.   State the advantages of a box-and-pan brake over a standard hand brake.

   1. _____

   _____

   _____

2.   What are four of the many objects that can be made on a box-and-pan brake?

   2. _____

   _____

   _____

   _____

3.   List the major parts of a box-and-pan brake.

   3. _____

   _____

   _____

   _____

4.   State the finger widths provided as standard equipment for a box-and-pan brake.

   4. _____

   _____

5.   List the adjustments that can be made on a box-and-pan brake.

   5. _____

   _____

   _____

   _____

6.   Universal hand brakes can be obtained in what standard bending lengths?

   6. _____

   _____

7.   Name the major parts of a universal hand brake.

   7. _____

   _____

   _____

   _____

   _____

8. List three nose bar attachments used on a universal hand brake.

8. _____

_____

_____

B. Insert the correct word or phrase in the following:

1. The box-and-pan brake differs from the standard hand brake in that the solid _____ bar is replaced by removable sectional _____

2. Fingers are made of _____ bars for maximum strength.

3. Fingers are adjusted or removed by _____ and _____ the thumbscrew.

4. The difference between a standard construction and optional construction box-and-pan brake is that the standard model has a _____ bottom bar and the optional model has a _____ bottom bar.

5. The capacity of a universal hand brake is _____ mild steel or _____ stainless steel.

6. Internal _____ can be formed on a universal hand brake.

7. The proper use of nose, bottom, and insert bars means that _____ can be formed on only one part of a sheet while leaving the remainder of the sheet flat.

C. Underline the correct word or phrase in the following:

1. The purpose of a box-and-pan brake is to form a box or pan from (several, one, two) sheet(s) of metal.

2. To form a box 12 in. x 12 in. x 6 in. with a standard set of fingers, a combination of (4 and 6; 3, 4 and 6; 3, 4, 5 and 6)-inch fingers will be used.

3. Inside corners on boxes or cabinets are formed with (radius nose fingers, standard width fingers, extension fingers).

4. To form triangular, square, tapered, and rectangular tubes, (radius nose, standard, extension, open-end) fingers are used.

5. In making a box, fingers must be set to the exact inside dimensions for the (hems, flanges, laps, opposite sides).

6. A (low radius, high radius, standard angle) bar is used to form a 2-inch radius bend.

7. To form a one-piece box 8 in. x 12 in. x 4 in., a(an) (low nose, high nose, insert) bar is used.

8. To bend 50 pieces at the same angle, the (top leaf, quadrant gage, insert bar) is adjusted and set.

UNIT 9 THROATLESS COMBINATION ROTARY MACHINES

OBJECTIVES

After studying this unit, the student will be able to

- Name the major parts of the throatless combination rotary machine.

- List the operations that can be made on the throatless rotary machine.

- Make the proper adjustments and use the throatless rotary machine.

The *throatless combination rotary machine* is provided with interchangeable rolls which enable the machine to perform turning, burring, wiring, elbow edging, flanging, and flattening operations. Figure 9-1 shows the machine with several commonly used rolls. This machine and the several variations of it to be covered in this unit all can be attached to a metal standard provided by the manufacturer. The standard then can be clamped to a bench.

The machine has a solid steel frame enclosing a series of quietly-operating gears that control the direction of rotation of the *arbors*. An arbor is an axle-type holder for the rolls. It is not necessary to alter the normal clockwise handle rotation to change the direction of rotation of the arbors. The throatless combination rotary machine has a 2-inch distance between shaft centers and a capacity of 22-gage mild steel. Power-driven machines are available for turning 18-gage steel.

TURNING MACHINE

When the throatless rotary machine is fitted with rolls as in figures 9-1 and 9-2, it is called a *turning machine.* The rolls are made of heat-treated steel and are screwed on the threaded ends of the shafts. The rolls can be removed with the special wrench supplied with the machine. The upper roll is disc-shaped with a rounded edge; the lower roll is cylindrically-shaped with a semicircular groove near the outer edge, figure 9-2. The upper roll is moved by a crankscrew and forms the edge on the job by pressing it into the groove in the lower roll. The alignment of the rolls is adjusted by a knurled nut at the end of the shaft.

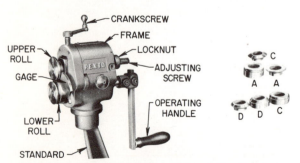

Fig. 9-1 Throatless combination rotary machine and rolls.
(Courtesy of The Peck, Stow & Wilcox Co.)

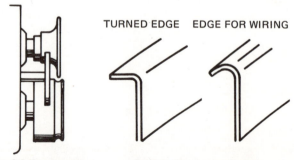

Fig. 9-2 Turning rolls

Fig. 9-3 Two types of edges

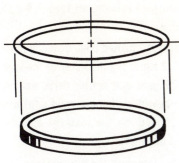

Fig. 9-4 Edge turned up

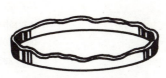

Fig. 9-5 Wavy edge

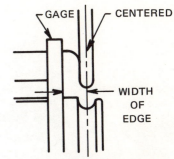

Fig. 9-6 Edge width and roll alignment

Two standard sets of turning rolls are available; one set will form an edge to take 11-gage wire (1/8 inch), and the other set will form an edge for 7-gage wire (3/16 inch).

Uses

The turning machine is used to form a narrow edge or flange on circular jobs; this edge has a small radius, figure 9-3. If the edge projects at a 90-degree angle from the job, it can be used for a double seam. If the edge is turned beyond 90 degrees, it can be used for wiring or stiffening, figure 9-3.

When the turning machine is used to make a slight impression on the edge of a job, the operation is called *creasing* or *scoring*. A circular job which is to be flanged by hand generally is creased first.

When an outer edge is turned on a disc, the diameter of the disc becomes smaller, figure 9-4, resulting in excess material which must be taken up. If the edge is narrow and the turning machine is operated correctly, the excess material is distributed so that the edge is even. This action is called *shrinking metal*. As the diameter becomes larger, the width of the edge that can be turned increases.

A turned edge with an uneven or wavy appearance has not been turned properly. Uneven edges result because the edge is too large, the work is unsteady, or it is raised too fast while it is being turned, figure 9-5.

A wider edge can be turned on a cylinder than on a disc because the cylinder edge is stretched instead of being compressed as on the disc. Edges turned for double seams should be narrow.

ADJUSTMENTS

The width of the turned edge is determined by the distance from the face of the gage to the center of the flange of the upper roll, figure 9-6. The gage is adjusted by a knurled screw and is held in place with a knurled locknut. The gage on some machines is located on the opposite side of the rolls so that the work can feed away from the operator.

HOW TO USE THE TURNING MACHINE

The sheet metal student must develop judgment and a sense of feel in using a turning machine to be able to know how much to turn the crankscrew for the various gages of material and how much to raise the job after each revolution to form a good edge. The arbors must be rotated so that the work touches the gage before passing through the rolls. Scoring or creasing should be done on the turning machine as there is less danger of cutting the metal than on the burring machine. The turning machine should be lubricated periodically, depending on the amount of use.

HOW TO PREPARE AN EDGE FOR WIRING

1. If the flange of the upper roll is not centered in the groove of the lower roll, center the rolls by adjusting the knurled nut at the end of the shaft, figure 9-1.

2. Set the gage for the width of the edge required by adjusting the knurled screw at the end of the gage. At the same time, use a rule to measure from the gage to the center of the edge of the upper roll, figure 9-7, page 62.

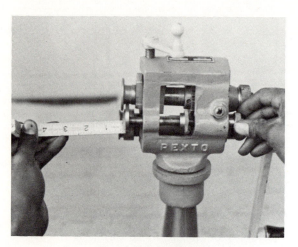

Fig. 9-7 Setting the gage

Fig. 9-8 Adjusting the upper roll

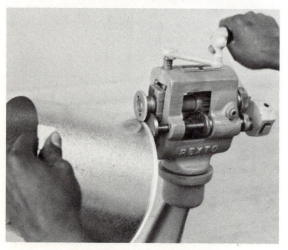

Fig. 9-9 Start of the edge for wire

In figure 9-7, the gage is being set for a 1/4-inch wide turned edge.

For a wired edge, the turned edge distance must be equal to 2 1/2 times the diameter of the wire for metal of 24 gage and lighter thickness. A line showing the width of the turned edge can be drawn or scribed on the material and the gage set for this distance.

3. Lock the gage in place with the knurled locknut.

4. Hold the job in the left hand and place the edge to be turned between the rolls and against the gage in a position slightly above horizontal, figure 9-8.

   Do not allow the work to fall below a horizontal position.

5. Turn the crankscrew with the right hand to lower the upper roll until it makes a slight impression on the metal, figure 9-8.

6. Hold the edge of the job against the gage with the left hand and turn the operating handle with the right hand until the entire edge of the job has passed through the rollers.

   CAUTION   Keep your fingers away from the rolls. Do not wear hanging jewelry or loose clothing while working at the machine. Keep long hair fastened and out of the way so that it does not become entangled in the machine.

   On the machine shown in figures 9-7 and 9-8, the job touches the gage before it passes through the rolls.

7. Lower the upper roll slightly by turning the crankscrew.

8. Raise the job slightly and turn the operating handle to make another complete turn around the job, figure 9-9. Edges can be turned on discs using this procedure.

9. Lower the upper roll again and complete the edge. Turn the operating handle and raise the job gradually after each complete revolution of the job until the required edge is obtained, figure 9-10.

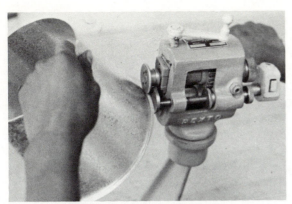

Fig. 9-10 Finish of edge for wire

Fig. 9-11 Scored edge (outside radius)

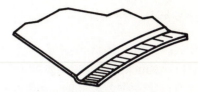

Fig. 9-12 Scored edge (inside radius)

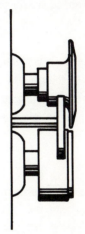

Fig. 9-13 Burring rolls

On light material the job may become deformed. Pull the job into shape as it passes through the machine.

10.   Loosen the crankscrew and remove the job.

SCORING OR CREASING

When using the gage for a job with an outside radius, figure 9-11, the edge is scored only, not turned.   The procedure is similar to preparing an edge for wiring.

If an inside radius is to be scored and the gage is not to be used, mark the edge to be scored, figure 9-12, set the gage back, and follow the mark by sight.

BURRING MACHINE

When the throatless rotary machine is fitted with rolls as in figures 9-1, page 60, and 9-13, it is called a *burring machine*.   The rolls are made of heat-treated steel and are screwed on the threaded ends of the shafts.   The upper roll is disc-shaped while the lower roll is cylindrical and has a recess near the outer end, figure 9-13.   The upper roll is adjusted by a crankscrew to clamp the metal while the edge is being burred.   The alignment of the rolls is adjusted by a knurled screw at the end of the shaft.

The capacity of the burring machine is 22-gage mild steel.   The maximum burr on an edge is 1/4 inch wide.   Power-driven machines are available to burr heavy-gage metal.

Burred Edges Versus Turned Edges

A turning machine makes an edge with a rounded radius, while the burring machine produces an edge with a sharp radius.   Because of the sharp radius, the burred edge must be made narrower than a turned edge on the same size disc to avoid a wavy edge.   In a similar manner, burred edges must be narrower on small-diameter discs than on large-diameter discs.   On small, light work, burred edges should not be over 1/8 inch wide.   A wider edge can be burred on a cylinder than on a disc.   Burred edges should be made narrower when used for double seaming.

Uses

The burring machine is used to form narrow edges on discs, covers, cylinders, and irregular pieces,

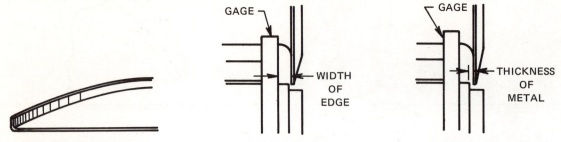

Fig. 9-14 Burred edge   Fig. 9-15 Gage setting   Fig. 9-16 Spacing of rolls

figure 9-14. Burred edges may be used for double seams, set-in bottoms, and Pittsburgh locks. A burring machine is also called a thin-edge machine. The burring machine can be used to score and crease material if care is taken not to cut the job.

ADJUSTMENTS

The width of the burr is determined by the distance from the face of the gage to the inner edge of the upper roll, figure 9-15. The gage is moved by a knurled screw and is held in place with a knurled locknut.

Aligning The Rolls

The rolls must be spaced properly for the specific job. The distance from the inner edge of the upper roll to the shoulder of the lower roll must be equal to the thickness of the metal to be burred, figure 9-16. The spacing is adjusted with the knurled nut at the end of the shaft.

Operation

The burring machine is the most difficult of the rotary machines to operate. To produce an evenly-burred edge, the job must be held in the proper position and the rolls must be turned at the proper speed. The rolls are rotated so that the work is fed from the gage side of the machine. Do not tighten the crank-screw too much at a time because this will result in cutting the burred edge. A burred edge should be made as narrow as possible; a wide edge is difficult to make and often must be straightened.

To make a good burred edge, turn the operating handle rapidly after the first revolution of the job,

Fig. 9-17 Setting the gage

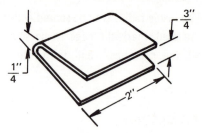

Fig. 9-18 Hand guard

hold the work steady, and do not raise the job too quickly.

HOW TO BURR A DISC

1. Place one end of the rule against the gage. Turn the knurled adjusting screw until the distance between the gage and the inner edge of the upper roll is equal to the width of the burr required. In figure 9-17, the gage is being set for a burr 1/8 inch wide.

A line showing the width of the burred edge required can be drawn or scribed on the disc.

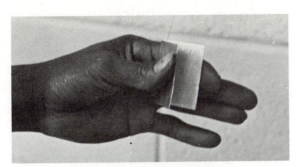

Fig. 9-19 Metal guard in hand

The gage is then set for this distance by holding the disc against the gage.

Fig. 9-20 Adjusting the upper roll

2. Lock the gage in place with the knurled locknut.

CAUTION To protect your hand from the sharp edge of the job and to assure that the job will turn freely in the hand, use a hand guard (a small piece of metal bent in a U-shape) between the job and your hand. Figure 9-18 shows a hand guard with approximate dimensions.

Fig. 9-21 Start of burring

3. Grasp the hand guard between the thumb and the first finger of the left hand, figure 9-19.

4. Holding the disc and hand guard in the left hand, place the edge to be burred between the rolls and against the gage in a position slightly above horizontal, figure 9-20. The disc must be circular and not have straight sides or sharp points.

5. Lower the upper roll by turning the crankscrew with the right hand until the metal is held firmly between the rolls, figure 9-20. Remember that tightening the crankscrew too much will cut the edge of the disc.

Fig. 9-22 Finish of burring

6. Figure 9-21 shows another method of holding a disc.

7. Hold the disc against the part of the gage between the rolls and turn the operating handle to allow the disc to pass freely through the guard, figure 9-21. Keep the guard between the hand and the edge of the revolving disc to avoid injury.

8. After the disc makes one complete revolution, raise it slightly. Rotate the disc another com-

plete turn and again raise the disc. Continue this procedure until the edge is burred to the position required, figure 9-22.

The operating handle should be turned rapidly to prevent a wavy edge.

Small discs which buckled during turning can be straightened by throwing them on a flat surface with the burred edge upward. If the disc is large or the edge is wavy, it can be straightened with a hammer and dolly.

HOW TO BURR AN EDGE ON A CYLINDER

1. Set the gage for the required width of the burr by turning the knurled adjustment screw.

2. Lock the gage in place with the knurled locknut.

Fig. 9-23 Burring a cylinder

Fig. 9-24 Finished burred edge on a cylinder

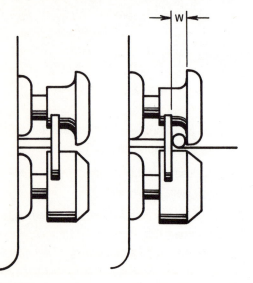

Fig. 9-25 Wiring rolls   **Fig. 9-26 Width adjustment**

3. Hold the job in the left hand and place the edge to be burred between the rolls and against the gage. The job must be held in a position slightly above horizontal.

4. Lower the upper roll by turning the crankscrew with the right hand until the metal is held firmly between the rolls. The burring rolls should not be tightened too much or they will cut the edge of the material.

5. Hold the edge of the job against the gage with the left hand and turn the operating handle with the right hand. The job should revolve freely between the thumb and fingers, figure 9-23. The job must be held firmly against the gage until the burred edge is finished.

6. After each complete revolution of the job, raise the job slightly with the left hand while continuing to turn the operating handle with the right hand. Continue this procedure until the edge is burred to the angle required, figure 9-24.

7. Loosen the crankscrew and remove the job. Tapered jobs are burred using the same procedure.

WIRING MACHINE

When the throatless rotary machine is fitted with the rolls shown in figure 9-25, it is called a *wiring machine*. The methods of mounting the rolls on the machine and aligning the rolls are similar to those given for the turning machine. The wiring machine is used to close the turned edge of a job over a wire.

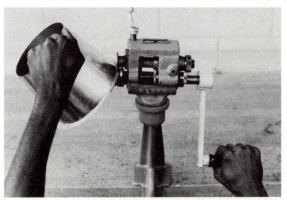

Fig. 9-27 Preparing wiring edge

Fig. 9-28 Retaining wire temporarily

Fig. 9-29 Completing wired edge

Adjustments

The width (W) between the inner edge of the upper roll and the gage is adjusted so that the edge of the upper roll clears the outer edge of the wire by a distance equal to two times the metal thickness, figure 9-26.

HOW TO USE THE WIRING MACHINE

1. Prepare the wiring edge of the job in the turning machine, figure 9-27.

2. Form the wire to the shape of the job by running the straight length of wire through the groove in the rolls of the slip-roll forming machine.

3. Place the formed wire in the turned edge of the job.

4. The wire can be held temporarily in position by closing the groove in several places with a mallet, figure 9-28.

5. Adjust the gage of the wiring machine so that the upper roll clears the outer edge of the wire, figure 9-26.

6. Place the job with the wire in place between the rolls.

7. Turn the crankscrew clockwise to lower the upper roll just enough to start turning the edge.

8. Hold the work in a horizontal position and rotate the edge through the rolls.

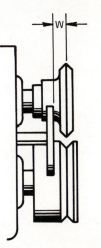

Fig. 9-30 Elbow edging rolls

9. Raise the job until it is slightly above a horizontal position, depress the upper roll, and repeat the operation until the metal is formed closely around the wire, figure 9-29.

ELBOW EDGING MACHINE

When the throatless rotary machine is fitted with the rolls shown in figure 9-30, it is known as an *elbow edger.*

The rolls, mounting methods, and roll alignment procedure are similar to those covered previously for the turning machine.

Uses

The elbow edger is used to form the impression or crease in the circular edge of elbows which enables

Fig. 9-31 Elbow section showing lock

Fig. 9-32 Setting the gage

corresponding sections to lock together, figure 9-31. The edger is used extensively in small sheet metal shops to make elbows of special sizes.

Adjustments

The gage setting is determined by the distance (W) from the face of the gage to the center of the flange of the upper roll, figure 9-30. The gage is adjusted with the knurled adjusting screw. On some machines the gage is on the opposite side; in these cases, the work feeds away from the operator.

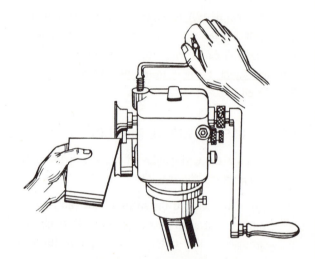

Fig. 9-33 Adjusting the upper roll

HOW TO USE THE ELBOW EDGING MACHINE

1. If the upper roll is not centered in the V groove of the lower roll, center the rolls by adjusting the knurled nut at the end of the shaft.

2. Set the gage for the required edge allowance by adjusting the knurled screw at the end of the gage while measuring from the gage to the center of the flange of the upper roll, figure 9-32. This edge allowance equals the groove width divided by 2 plus 1/16 inch: $A = (W \div 2) + 1/16$ inch.

3. Lock the gage in place with the knurled locknut.

Fig. 9-34 Turning the elbow edge

4. Hold the job in the left hand and place the edge to be turned between the rolls and against the gage in a horizontal position, figure 9-33.

5. Lower the upper roll by turning the crankscrew with the right hand until the roll makes an impression on the metal, figure 9-33.

6. Hold the edge of the job against the gage with the left hand and turn the operating handle with the right hand until one complete revolution of the job is made.

7. Lower the upper roll slightly by turning the crankscrew.

8. Make another complete revolution of the job by turning the operating handle, figure 9-34.

9. Lower the upper roll again and complete the edge by turning the operating handle until the desired edge is obtained.

Fig. 9-35 Turning corresponding elbow section

10. Loosen the crankscrew and remove the job.

11. To form corresponding sections, follow the procedure outlined in steps 1 to 10, and hold the section as shown in figure 9-35.

SUMMARY REVIEW

A. Place your answers to the following questions in the column to the right.

1. List three operations that can be accomplished on a throatless combination rotary machine.

1. _____
   _____
   _____

2. Name the parts of a throatless combination rotary machine.

2. _____
   _____
   _____
   _____
   _____
   _____
   _____
   _____

3. List two uses for a turned edge.

3. _____
   _____

4. What are three types of jobs that require a burred edge?

4. _____
   _____
   _____

5. List three seams that require a burred edge.

5. _____
   _____
   _____

6. List the three general requirements necessary to make a good burred edge.

    6. _____

       _____

       _____

B. Insert the correct word or phrase in the following:

1. The throatless combination rotary machine has a capacity of _____ -gage metal.

2. The edge formed with a turning machine has a small _____ .

3. When only a slight impression is made with the turning machine on the edge of a job, the operation is called _____ or _____ .

4. The rolls on a turning machine should be adjusted for the _____ of the edge and _____ .

5. The maximum burr on the edge of a piece of stock is _____ inch.

6. The burring machine is commonly called a(an) _____ machine.

7. The purpose of a wiring machine is to _____ the turned edge on a piece of sheet metal over a _____ .

8. The clearance between the upper roll and the wire should be _____ the metal thickness.

9. The elbow edging machine is used to form the _____ in the circular edge of elbows.

10. When round elbows of _____ sizes are made, the elbow edging machine is very useful.

C. Underline the correct word or phrase in the following:

1. Rolls (slip, screw) on the (threaded, keyed) ends of the shafts on the throatless rotary machine.

2. The (lower, upper) roll is moved by the crankscrew.

3. A sharp 90-degree flange, 1/8 inch wide, is made on a (turning, burring, wiring) machine.

4. A burred edge is always made as (wide, narrow, straight) as possible.

5. A good burred edge is made by turning the operating handle (evenly, slowly, rapidly) after the (first, second, third) revolution.

6. When the elbow edger is used, the work is held in the (right, left) hand and the handle is turned with the (left, right) hand.

7. Too tight an adjustment of the upper roll will result in (cutting, creasing, bending) the metal during the burring procedure.

UNIT 10 DEEP THROAT COMBINATION ROTARY MACHINES

OBJECTIVES

After studying this unit, the student will be able to

- List the parts of the deep throat combination rotary machine.

- State the uses of the deep throat combination rotary machine.

- Demonstrate the correct procedures for adjusting and using the deep throat combination rotary machine to bead, crimp, and edge a furnace collar.

The *deep throat combination rotary machine* with sets of interchangeable rolls can perform all of the operations possible with the throatless combination rotary machine, with the addition of beading, crimping, and furnace collar edging operations.

The deep throat combination rotary machine, figure 10-1, has a 24-gage capacity (a 26-gage capacity for crimping only), a 7-inch throat, and a 2-inch distance between shaft centers.

BEADING MACHINE

The *beading machine* is used to roll curved impressions in metal. The frame of the machine is mounted on a bench standard and held in place by a setscrew. The roll shafts project beyond the frame and are connected by gears enclosed by the frame. The lower roll shaft rotates in and is supported by a horn extending from the frame. This horn allows beads to be formed at a considerable distance from the edge of the work.

The rolls are available in pairs and are made of hardened steel. They fit over keys on the shafts and are held in place with circular nuts. The nuts, each of which has two holes near the outside edge on opposite sides of the diameter, are removed with a special wrench supplied with the machine. The roll sets are

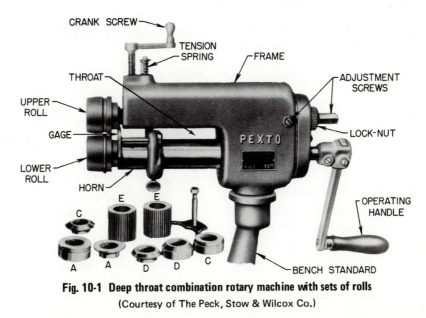

Fig. 10-1 Deep throat combination rotary machine with sets of rolls
(Courtesy of The Peck, Stow & Wilcox Co.)

71

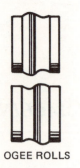
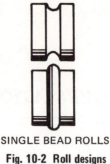
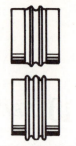

OGEE ROLLS

SINGLE BEAD ROLLS

TRIPLE BEAD ROLLS

Fig. 10-2 Roll designs

available in three designs, figure 10-2, to form single beads, ogee beads, and triple beads, figure 10-3. The upper roll of the machine is raised and lowered by means of a crankscrew.

Also available for use on heavy gage metal and in heating and ventilating work are hand-operated machines and power-driven machines.

Uses

A beading machine rolls curved impressions or *beads* in metal. Beads strengthen and ornament sheet metal surfaces. The most commonly used beads are the single bead, the ogee bead, and the triple bead, figure 10-3. The beading operation also is known as *swaging*.

Beads

The *single bead* is a single curved impression which is usually formed on the outside of the job, but may be formed on the inside of the job if required, figure 10-3A. As the most frequently used bead, the single bead is used as a stop on pipes, tanks, and drums to prevent one part of the job from sliding into the other part. This type of bead is also used to strengthen or ornament tanks and drums.

The *ogee bead* consists of a double bead; one part of the bead is on the outside of the job and the other part of the bead is on the inside, figure 10-3B. Ogee beads are used in the same manner as single beads.

The *triple bead* consists of a group of three beads on the same side of the sheet, figure 10-3C. The outer beads are smaller than the center bead. The triple bead is used to ornament and stiffen round and flaring tinware.

A. OGEE BEAD

B. SINGLE BEAD

C. TRIPLE BEAD

Fig. 10-3 Bead types

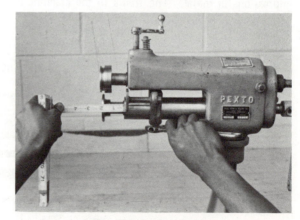

Fig. 10-4 Setting the gage

GAGE ADJUSTMENT

The distance between the bead and the edge of the work is regulated by adjusting the gage of the

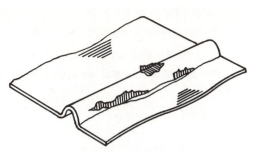

Fig. 10-5 Results of incorrect beading

Fig. 10-6 Removing the circular nut

Fig. 10-7 Unequal clearances

machine, figure 10-4. The gage is fitted to the horn on the lower shaft and is held rigidly in the proper position with a thumbscrew. The large, polished face of the gage guides the work.

1. Using a rule or scale, set the gage to the desired distance from the bead. In figure 10-4, the gage is being set for a distance of 1 3/4 inches between the edge of the bead and the edge of the job.

2. When the gage is set, turn the thumbscrew clockwise to fasten the gage securely in position.

HOW TO PRODUCE A GOOD BEAD

The beading machine is easy to operate; however, good beads are the result of the following three factors.

- The work must be held against the gage for the first revolution.

- The bead must not cross a seam.

- The upper roll must be lowered gradually.

The forming of the complete bead in one operation strains the metal with the result that it will separate or the coating on the metal will flake, figure 10-5.

Damage to the protective coating on the metal or cracks in the metal will result in corrosion of the metal if the job is exposed to moist conditions or corrosive fumes.

HOW TO CHANGE THE ROLLS OF A BEADING MACHINE

1. Raise the upper roll with the crankscrew.

2. Using the special wrench provided with the machine, place the two prongs into the holes of

the nut located at the front of the upper roll, figure 10-6.

3. Hold the operating handle with the right hand and loosen the upper circular nut with the wrench. The nut can be removed by turning the wrench or the crank handle.

CAUTION Press your index finger on the pronged end of the wrench so that it will not slip and cause personal injury or damage the metal.

4. Remove the upper roll by sliding it off the end of the shaft.

5. Repeat steps 2 through 4 for the lower roll.

6. Place the desired rolls on the machine by installing first the lower roll and then the upper roll. The keyway in each roll must fit over the key on the shaft.

7. Check the alignment of the rolls by lowering the upper roll with the crankscrew until it just touches the lower roll. The clearance on each

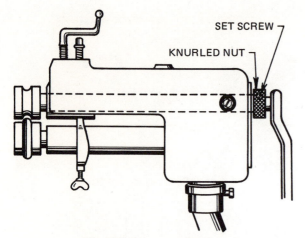

Fig. 10-8 Clearance adjustment

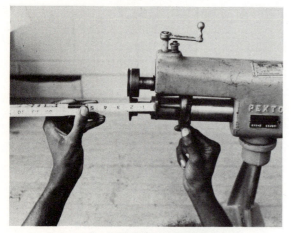

Fig. 10-9 Setting the gage

Fig. 10-10 Lowering upper roll by tightening the crankscrew

side of the bead should be equal. If the clear-ances are not equal, figure 10-7, page 73, use the following procedure to adjust the knurled nut at the end of the crankshaft.

a. Loosen the setscrew in the knurled nut with an appropriate screwdriver, figure 10-8.

b. Turn the knurled nut on the crankshaft until the clearance is equal on each side of the bead.

c. Tighten the setscrew.

HOW TO MAKE A BEAD

1. Select the proper set of rolls for a single, ogee, or triple bead. Install the rolls on the machine.

2. Set the gage on the lower shaft of the machine to the desired distance. In figure 10-9, the gage is being set for a distance of 1 3/4 inches be-tween the edge of the bead and the edge of the job. The desired distance may be from the gage to the center of the bead or from the gage to the edge of the bead.

3. Fasten the gage with the thumbscrew.

4. Check the alignment of the upper and lower rolls.

5. Insert the work between the rolls with the edge of the metal pressed firmly against the gage.

6. Hold the work in a horizontal position with the left hand. Using the crankscrew on the top of the machine, lower the upper roll with the right hand until the work is held firmly between the rolls, figure 10-10. Be careful not to lower the upper roll too much for each succeeding revolution of the work to prevent cutting the metal or marring the surface of the job.

7. Hold the work against the gage with the left hand and turn the operating handle with the right hand. The work should pass easily between the thumb and fingers of the left hand, fig-ure 10-11.

Note: The work must touch the gage before it passes through the rolls.

The bead should be made in several revolutions of the work. A greater number of revolutions is necessary to achieve the required depth of the bead

Fig. 10-11 Starting the bead

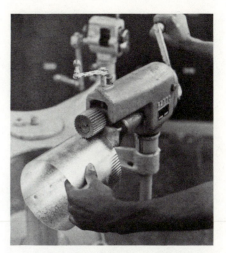

Fig. 10-12 Crimping machine

Fig. 10-13 Combination bead and crimp

on heavy metal. The seam of the job must not pass between the rolls; either raise the upper roll or reverse the machine.

CAUTION — Keep fingers away from the rolls. Do not wear long hair, hanging jewelry, and loose clothing while working at the machine.

8. Lower the upper roll slightly and repeat steps 6 and 7 until the required depth of bead is obtained.

    As the bead deepens, the work will draw away from the gage.

9. Raise the upper roll using the crankscrew and remove the work.

CRIMPING MACHINE

When the deep throat combination rotary machine is fitted with *crimping rolls*, figure 10-12, it is known as a *crimping machine*. The operating handle is usually lengthened to obtain the extra leverage required for crimping.

The standard roller equipment consists of one pair of crimping rolls, a pair of ogee beading rolls, and a pair of spacing collars which replace the beading rolls when the work is to be crimped only. The rolls are made of hardened steel. They fit over the keys on the shafts and are held in place with nuts countersunk flush with the shaft ends. The crimping rolls are slightly tapered at the outer ends to prevent the metal from being torn at the end of the crimped edge. The corrugations on the crimping rolls may be straight or spiraled. It is possible to make a bead and crimp the material at the same time if the beading rolls are installed at the ends of the crimping rolls, figure 10-13.

Crimping

Crimping is the process of corrugating sheet metal and at the same time contracting it. Crimping is usually done by machine in the sheet metal shop. A hand crimper can be used at the job site. The diameter of a pipe is made smaller when the end is crimped. This procedure eliminates the need for laying out a large and a small end on the same section of pipe, and thus simplifies the connection of sections of pipe.

ADJUSTMENTS

The width of the crimp can be regulated by adjusting the gage, figure 10-14, page 76. The gage is clamped in place by a wingscrew. The depth of the

Fig. 10-14 Setting the gage

Fig. 10-15 Crimping

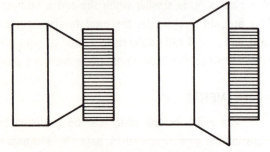

Fig. 10-16 Furnace collar edging rolls

crimp is regulated by raising or lowering the top roll using the crankscrew, figure 10-14. When using the beading and crimping rolls together to produce a deep bead and a light crimp, or a light bead and a deep crimp, the rolls may be tipped by adjusting the screws located on each side of the frame near the operating handle.

HOW TO CRIMP

A crimping machine is easy to use. However, the operator must be careful not to tighten the rolls so much that the material bulges at the end of the corrugations. If possible, the crimping should be done in one revolution of the work. The machine must be rotated so that the work touches the gage before passing through the rolls; the work must continue to touch the gage until the crimping operation is complete.

1. Raise the upper roll by turning the crankscrew.

2. Loosen the wingscrew, set the gage to the desired crimp width, and tighten the wingscrew. In figure 10-14, the gage is being set for a crimp 1 1/4 inches wide.

    For jobs with riveted or grooved seams, start the crimp beside the seam and finish without crossing the seam. The corrugations on the rolls can be damaged by crossing the seam of the job.

3. Place the edge to be crimped between the rolls and against the gage. The work must touch the gage at all times.

4. Lower the upper roll. Turn the crankscrew with the right hand until the desired depth of the crimp is obtained.

5. Hold the work in a horizontal position against the gage with the left hand. Turn the operating handle with the right hand. The work should pass easily between the thumb and fingers of the left hand, figure 10-15.

CAUTION   Keep your fingers away from the crimping rolls. Do not wear long hair, loose clothing, or hanging jewelry while working at the machine.

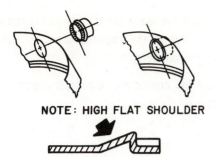

NOTE: HIGH FLAT SHOULDER

Fig. 10-17 Furnace collar edging

6. Raise the upper roll and remove the work.

How To Bead and Crimp at the Same Time

The ends of circular pipes can be beaded and crimped in one operation by installing both the ogee rolls and the crimping rolls on the machine.

1. Replace the spacing collars with the beading rolls. Put the beading rolls at the ends of the shafts after the crimping rolls.

2. Set the gage and the upper roll as in the crimping procedure.

3. Insert the work and perform the operations given in the crimping procedure.

FURNACE COLLAR EDGING MACHINE

The deep throat combination rotary machine can be fitted with a pair of furnace collar edging rolls; in this case, the machine is known as a *furnace collar edging machine.*

The rolls, figure 10-16, are made of hardened steel. The procedures for mounting and adjusting the rolls are similar to those given for the beading rolls.

The furnace collar edging machine is used on ductwork to make 90-degree connections similar to the dovetail seam, figure 10-18.

The rolls form a flat shoulder and crimp on the end of round pipe.

HOW TO USE THE FURNACE COLLAR EDGING MACHINE

1. Select the proper rolls and install them on the machine.

2. Set the gage on the lower shaft of the machine to the desired depth, figure 10-18. The gage should be next to the crimp part of the rolls but should not touch the rolls.

Fig. 10-18 Gage set at required depth

Fig. 10-19 Work firmly held against the gage

3. Fasten the gage with the setscrew, figure 10-18.

4. Check the alignment of the upper and lower rolls. If the clearances are not equal, adjust the knurled nut at the end of the crankshaft until the clearances are equal.

5. Insert the work between the rolls with the edge pressed firmly against the gage.

6. Hold the work in a horizontal position with the left hand. Turn the crankscrew on top of the machine with the right hand to lower the upper roll until the work is held firmly between the rolls, figure 10-19.

CAUTION If the upper roll is lowered too much for each succeeding revolution of the work, the rolls may cut the metal or the surface of the job may be marred.

7. Hold the work against the gage with the left hand and turn the operating handle with the right hand. The work should pass easily between the thumb and the fingers of the left hand.

The work must touch the gage before it passes through the rolls.

The collar edge should be made in several revolutions of the work. A greater number of revolutions are necessary to obtain the required depth of the collar edge on heavy metal.

8. Lower the upper roll slightly and repeat steps 6 and 7 until the required depth of the collar edge is obtained.

9. Use the crankscrew to raise the upper roll and remove the work.

SUMMARY REVIEW

A. Place your answers to the following questions in the column to the right.

1. Name three operations that can be performed on pipe with a deep throat combination rotary machine.

1. _____
    _____
    _____

2. List the parts of a deep throat combination rotary machine.

2. _____
    _____
    _____
    _____
    _____
    _____
    _____
    _____
    _____
    _____
    _____

3. What are the two general purposes for beads?

3. _____
    _____

4. What are the three types of beads?

4. _____
    _____
    _____

5. List three items on which a single bead is used as a stop.

5. _____
    _____
    _____

6. Name the standard roller equipment required to make a beaded and crimped pipe end.

6. _____
    _____
    _____

7. List two conditions necessary for a furnace collar edge.

7. _____
    _____

8. List two safety precautions that the sheet metal worker should observe when operating a rotary turning machine.

8. _____
    _____

B. Insert the correct word or phrase in the following:

1. The projecting _____ allows beads to be formed at a considerable distance from the _____ of the work.

2. Rolls are made of _____ steel and fit over _____ on the shaft of the machine.

3. The _____ bead is the most frequently used bead.

4. To make a good bead, it must not cross a(an) _____ .

5. The vertical movements of the upper roll are controlled by the _____ .

6. If the upper roll is turned down too much for any one revolution when making the bead, the metal may be _____ or the surface _____ .

7. Crimping is the process of _____ sheet metal edges.

8. In the crimping operation, the work must touch the _____ at all times.

9. The purpose of the furnace collar edging machine is to make a _____ to a duct.

10. If the bead is formed in one operation, the metal will be _____ .

C. Underline the correct word or phrase in the following:

1. Rolls are removed from the beading machine by loosening the circular nut with a (an) (Allen wrench, pipe wrench, special wrench).

2. Properly aligned rolls should have (equal, no, loose) clearance on each side of the bead.

3. When starting the bead, the work is held in a (vertical, angular, horizontal) position with the left hand.

4. To produce a deep bead and a light crimp, or a light bead and a deep crimp, the rolls should be (separated, straightened, tightened, tipped, loosened).

5. A bead should always be formed in (one, two, several) revolutions of the work.

UNIT 11 SPECIALTY TURNING MACHINES: EASY EDGER, DOUBLE SEAMING, AND SETTING DOWN MACHINES

OBJECTIVES

After studying this unit, the student will be able to

- List the major parts of the easy edger, double seaming, and setting down machines.

- Demonstrate the proper use of the easy edger, double seaming, and setting down machines.

Specialized turning machines perform specific operations in the sheet metal shop. Although many of these operations can be done by hand, many fabricating shops that make all their own fittings and production shops that make large quantities of the same items have replaced the hand operations with machines.

EASY EDGER

A flanging machine called the *easy edger* is used to make flanges for square or rectangular elbows, or flanges on other curved edge fittings. The easy

edger consists of a frame, operating handle, crankscrew, rolls, gage, bed, bench standard, and gear train, figure 11-1.

The heat-treated and hardened steel rolls are pinned to the ends of the shafts. The upper roll is V shaped with a sharp edge and the lower roll is groove shaped with a small shoulder gage on one side of the groove, figure 11-2. The shoulder gage is set permanently at 90 degrees to the inside edge of the lower roll.

The easy edger has a capacity of 20-gage mild steel. It will turn a 7/32-inch flange on a radius as small as 1 3/4 inches. Power-driven machines are available for turning heavier gage metal.

HOW TO USE THE EASY EDGER

The sheet metal student must practice using the easy edger to develop a sense of feel for the amount

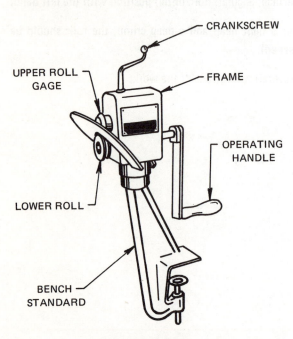

Fig. 11-1 Easy edger

CRANKSCREW

UPPER ROLL
GAGE

FRAME

OPERATING
HANDLE

LOWER ROLL

BENCH
STANDARD

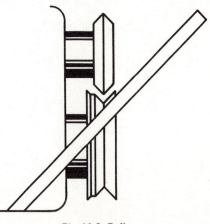

Fig. 11-2 Rolls

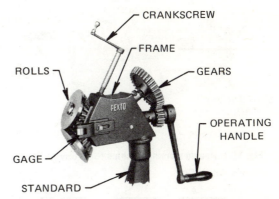

Fig. 11-3 Flange being formed (Courtesy of The Lockformer Company)

Fig. 11-4 Setting down machine (Courtesy of The Peck, Stow & Wilcox Co.)

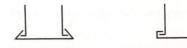

Fig. 11-5 Flanged section   **Fig. 11-6 Finished seam**

the crankscrew can be tightened for various gages of material. The machine must be rotated so that the work touches the shoulder gage on the lower roll before passing through the rolls.

1. Turn the crankscrew all the way down; then return the crankscrew approximately one-quarter turn.

2. Hold the job in your left hand and place the edge to be turned so that it rests against the shoulder gage and in the groove, figure 11-3.

3. Turn the operating handle and push the job to start it.

4. Adjust the crankscrew so that the upper roll is tight enough on the job to draw the material and leave a square corner.

5. Rotate the crankscrew with your right hand until the 90-degree flange is formed on the complete job. The edge may wrinkle on very small curves. If this wrinkling does occur, run the job through the rolls a second time. It may be necessary to tighten the crankscrew slightly. To obtain a flange that is satisfactory in height and form, the edge of the material must rest against the groove in the lower forming roll for the entire operation. If the job is not seated properly, the uneven pressure will cause an irregular height and a heavy wrinkle.

SETTING DOWN MACHINE

The *setting down machine*, figure 11-4, is used to finish and compress flanges on the bottoms and bodies of cans, pails, and covers. The flanges are formed on the burring machine and the sections fitted together before the setting down machine is used.

The setting down machine consists of a frame or housing, operating handle, crankscrew, rolls, gage, and gears. It has a capacity of 24-gage mild steel for seams up to 3/8 inch. A heavy–duty machine is available for 18-gage mild steel and seams up to 1/2 inch.

HOW TO USE THE SETTING DOWN MACHINE

1. Form the flanges on the sections to be seamed using the burring machine. Fit the sections together, figure 11-5. Tack the seam in several places with a mallet to hold the sections together.

2. Open the rolls of the setting down machine with the crankscrew. Set the seam flange between the rolls so that it rests against the gage.

3. Adjust the distance between the rolls to the approximate finished thickness of the seam and tighten the crankscrew.

4. Turn the operating handle with your right hand and hold the piece against the gage with the left hand until the seam is completed, figure 11-6.

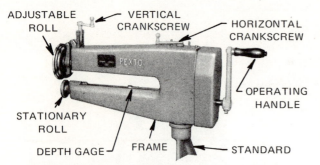
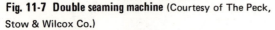

Fig. 11-7 Double seaming machine (Courtesy of The Peck, Stow & Wilcox Co.)

Fig. 11-8 Seaming operations (Courtesy of The Peck, Stow & Wilcox Co.)

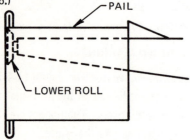

Fig. 11-9 Pail in position on lower roll

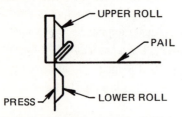

Fig. 11-10 Rolls adjusted for operation B (figure 11-8)

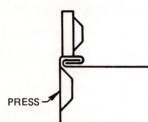

Fig. 11-11 Rolls adjusted for operation C (figure 11-8)

DOUBLE SEAMING MACHINE

The *double seaming machine*, figure 11-7, is used in many sheet metal shops that make quantities of items with double seams. This machine finishes the double seam after the preliminary flanges are made on the burring machine and the sections are fitted together. The seams of pails, cans, buckets, and any cylindrical body requiring a flat bottom can be finished on the double seaming machine.

The machine consists of a frame similar in design to that of the deep throat rotary machine, operating handle, crankscrews, rolls, depth gage, and gears. Like all of the other types of rotary machines, it is held in a standard clamped to a bench. The capacity of the machine is 26-gage mild steel. The maximum throat depth of the machine is 15 1/2 inches.

HOW TO USE THE DOUBLE SEAMING MACHINE

1. Using the burring machine, form the flanges on the sections to be seamed.

2. Fit the sections together by hand and tack in position with a mallet, figure 11-8A.

3. Turn the vertical crankscrew to open the rolls and slide the item to be seamed over the lower roll until it is in the position shown in figure 11-9.

4. Set the gage for the depth of the seam.

5. Use both of the crankscrews to adjust the top roll to the position shown in figure 11-10.

6. Turn the operating handle to complete the first seaming operation, figure 11-8B.

7. Use both crankscrews to readjust the top roll to the position shown in figure 11-11.

8. Turn the operating handle with your right hand and press on the bottom of the pail with your left hand until the seam is complete.

SUMMARY REVIEW

A. Place your answers to the following questions in the column to the right.

    1. Name three single-purpose rotary machines used in many shops.

    1. _____

    _____

    _____

2. List two types of shops that may use special-purpose machines.

2. _____

_____

3. List the parts of an easy edging machine.

3. _____

_____

_____

_____

_____

_____

_____

_____

4. List three items for which the setting down machine can be used to complete the bottom seam.

4. _____

_____

_____

B. Insert the correct word or phrase in the following:

1. The easy edger is used to make perfect _____ on square or rectangular elbows.

2. Rolls on all turning machines are _____ and _____ steel.

3. The shoulder gage on the easy edger is permanently set _____ to the inside.

4. The regular setting down machine has a capacity of _____ -gage mild steel for seams up to

_____ .

5. The double seaming machine can be used on any _____ body requiring a _____ bottom.

C. Underline the correct word or phrase in the following:

1. The double seaming machine has a capacity of (18, 20, 24, 26)-gage sheet metal.

2. The lower roll on a double seaming machine is (adjustable, stationary, removable).

3. When using the easy edger to turn a flange on a small radius curve, the material may (bend, warp, wrinkle).

4. The setting down machine is used to complete a (an) (Pittsburgh lock, single seam, double seam).

5. After flanging in the double seaming machine, the double seam is completed in (one, two, three) operations.

UNIT 12 TURRET PUNCH PRESS, METAL NOTCHER, AND ANGLE IRON MACHINE

OBJECTIVES

After studying this unit, the student will be able to

- List the parts of the turret punch press, metal notcher, and angle iron machine.

- Adjust each machine properly for the required job.

- Operate each machine properly and safely.

Sheet metal shops generally are equipped with hand-operated metal punching machines. Some shops may have power-operated machines instead of or in addition to the hand-operated machines. These machines punch holes of various shapes, including round, triangular, semicircular, square, rectangular, vee, and tee in sheet metal and plate.

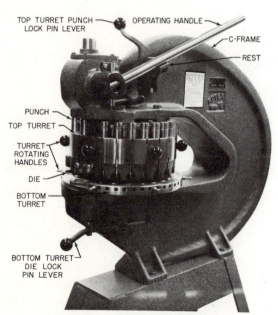

Fig. 12-1 Rotary turret punch press
(Courtesy of Rotex Punch Company, Inc.)

TURRET PUNCH PRESS

Figure 12-1 illustrates the *rotary turret punch press* which is a versatile machine with a variety of punch and die shapes and sizes. This machine is easily adaptable to any punching requirements for round or irregular holes.

The turret punch press consists of a cast iron frame, hardened steel punches and dies, quick turn turret knobs, alphabet indicators, and a safety lock. The size identification for each item is clearly marked on all of the various punches and dies.

The turret punch press in figure 12-1 has a capacity of 10-gage mild steel in the smaller punch sizes and 14-gage mild steel for the largest punch. The punch press has an 18-inch throat depth, and thus can punch to the center of a 36-inch wide sheet of material. Punch and die sets can be selected to fit the needs of the sheet metal shop; however, the standard selection consists of the following diameters of punches and dies: 5/32, 3/16, 7/32, 1/4, 9/32, 5/16, 3/8, 7/16, 1/2, 5/8, 3/4, 7/8, 1, 1 1/8, 1 1/4, 1 1/2, and 2 inches. The punch center has a small conical protrusion to provide for exact hole alignment.

HOW TO USE THE TURRET PUNCH PRESS

1. Place the operating handle in the rest position as shown in figure 12-1.

Fig. 12-2 Punching holes in metal strips
(Courtesy of Rotex Punch Company, Inc.)

2. Select the desired punch and die according to the size and lettering stamped on the punch holders and turrets.

3. Release the punch turret by pushing up on the lock pin lever of the top turret punch.

4. Rotate the top turret so that the hole punch of the desired size is in the front position.

5. Release the top turret punch lock pin lever.

6. Release the bottom die turret by pushing down on the lock pin lever of the bottom turret.

7. Rotate the bottom turret until the correct die size is aligned with the punch size selected in step 4. The letters on the die and punch turrets should coincide.

8. Release the bottom turret die lock pin lever.

9. Make a trial punch without material to check the alignment of the punch and die.

10. Mark the center of the hole location in the stock to be punched.

11. Line up the center punch mark on the stock with the punch centering pin on the machine.

12. Bring the operating handle forward to punch the hole, figure 12-2.

HOW TO REPLACE A PUNCH AND DIE

To replace the punch, line up the punch holder with the removable notch in the right side of the punch holder track; line up the largest die with the

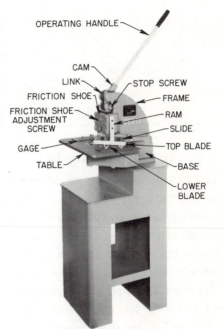

Fig. 12-3 Hand notcher
(Courtesy of The Peck, Stow & Wilcox Co.)

punch to be changed. Remove the notch and drop the punch and its holder through the die.

To remove the die, align it with the waste chute. Back off the setscrews in the die plate and lift the die up and out of the turret. The eccentric hole in the die allows adjustments to be made. After a die is replaced in the turret, reach under the lower turret to rotate the die in the socket while making trial strokes with the punch. A shim may be required to complete the alignment. When the die is properly aligned, tighten the setscrews.

COMBINATION NOTCHER, COPER, AND SHEARS

The *combination hand notcher, coper, and shears*, figure 12-3, is available either as a bench model or a floor model. This machine will make notches up to 6 in. x 6 in. x 90 degrees in 16-gage mild steel. It is actuated by an eccentric cam rolling on an aviation-type bearing. A press-type ram is aligned and held in place by 30-degree angle gibs. There is a 6-inch scale on each side of the lower 90-degree blade. In addition, an adjustable gage is mounted on the table on each side of the lower 90-degree blade to permit quick setups for duplicate notching.

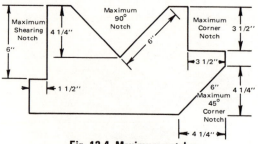

Fig. 12-4 Maximum notches

Various types of notches can be sheared. Figure 12-4 illustrates the maximum sizes for square corner, rectangular corner, 45-degree corner, and 90-degree corner notches.

Special box flange blades are available for trimming and notching a box or pan blank for easy forming. The lower blades are symmetrical and can be mounted to use all four cutting edges. The upper standard blades are factory set to make a cut starting at the apex or corner of an inside cut; this is known as *piece cutting*. By interchanging the upper blades, a *splay cut* can be made. This is a cut starting at the outside edge of sheet.

BLADE ADJUSTMENT

1. Unscrew the two table screws and remove the table.

2. Position the slide at the bottom of the stroke.

3. Loosen the lower blade bolts slightly.

4. Turn the lower blade adjusting screws so that there is a .002-inch clearance between the upper blade and the lower blade. The clearance should be greater for heavy stock than for thin stock.

5. Tighten the blade bolts securely.

6. Remount the table.

Other Adjustments

1. The depth of the cut can be limited by adjusting the stop screw.

2. The throat can be opened by backing off the frame bolt.

3. The safety brake should be adjusted using the friction shoe adjustment screw to prevent the deadweight fall of the handle and slide.

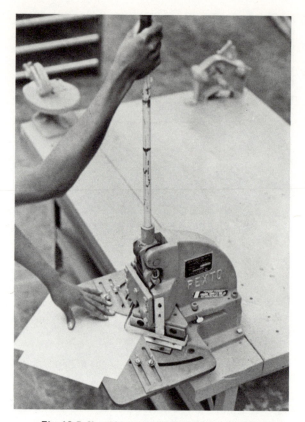

Fig. 12-5 Notching corners using the hand notcher

4. The slide can be adjusted to compensate for wear with the slide cap screws.

5. The gage can be set using the combination square. The table edges are machined at a 45-degree angle to the cutting edges.

HOW TO USE THE HAND METAL NOTCHER

1. Move the operating handle to the position shown in figure 12-3. In this position, the punch opens to its maximum height.

2. Set the stop to the depth of cut desired.

3. Set the gage to the size of the notch required.

4. Locate the center of the notch on the material to be cut and scribe a centerline.

5. Place the stock under the punch so that the scribed centerline coincides with the vertex of the angle of the punch.

6. Pull the lever forward to complete the notch, figure 12-5.

Fig. 12-6 Combination angle iron machine
(Courtesy of The Peck, Stow & Wilcox Co.)

Fig. 12-7 Angle iron shears
(Courtesy of The Whitney Metal Tool Co.)

ANGLE IRON COMBINATION MACHINE

The *combination angle iron machine*, figure 12-6, can be used in the shop as well as at the job site. This machine has a capacity of 2 x 2 x 1/4-inch angle iron.

ANGLE IRON SHEARS

The angle iron shears, figure 12-7, is used to shear angle iron up to a maximum size of 2 x 2 x 1/4 inches. When a standard movable shears blade is used, a distortion of one leg of the angle iron occurs. The distortion can be corrected by striking the leg several times with a hammer. However, distortion does not occur when a contour movable shears blade is used. Contour blades can be used only on angle iron with equal flanges up to a thickness of 3/16 inch.

One type of angle iron shears makes a double cut and does not distort either leg of the angle iron. This machine cuts out of the angle a 3/8-inch section which becomes scrap. Only equal flange angle iron can be cut using this machine. The use of unequal flange angle iron will damage the blade.

HOW TO USE THE ANGLE IRON SHEARS

1. Fit the machine with a 72-inch long operating handle, figure 12-8.

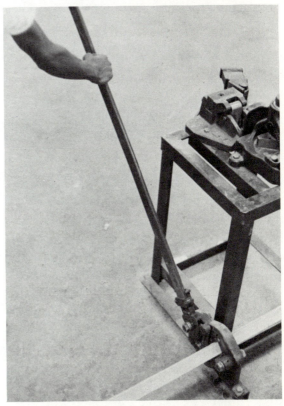

Fig. 12-8 Cutting angle iron in the shears

2. Open the blades to their full width.

3. Slide the angle iron to be cut between the blades until the marked length coincides with the stationary cutting blade edge.

Fig. 12-9 Adjusting the angle iron to the proper height

4.   Level the angle iron by adjusting the screw on the horizontal rod, figure 12-9.

5.   Pull the handle in a counterclockwise direction until the angle is cut.

ANGLE IRON NOTCHER

The *angle iron notcher*, figure 12-10, also is used to shear angle iron. This machine can make a 90-degree notch in one flange of an angle iron, a notch of any desired angle using a special die and notching blade, or can cope the flange as shown in figure 12-11. The angle iron notcher has a 32-inch operating bar handle and a capacity of 2 x 2 x 1/4-inch angle iron. Heavy-duty machines can shear 3 x 3 x 3/8-inch angle iron. The machine can be mounted on an angle iron mounting stand available from the manufacturer.

HOW TO USE THE ANGLE IRON NOTCHER

1.   Open the adjusting block by rotating the fluted knob counterclockwise.

2.   Raise the notching blade by rotating the operating bar handle counterclockwise. Use the 32-inch bar if needed.

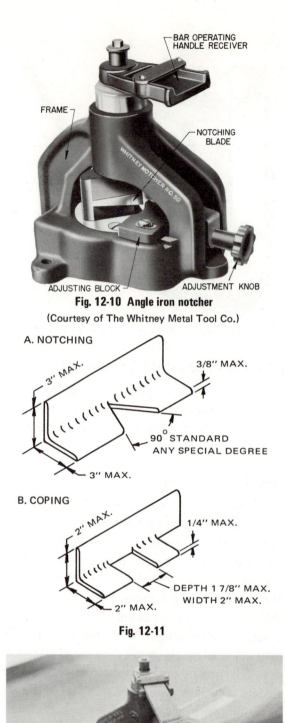

Fig. 12-10 Angle iron notcher

(Courtesy of The Whitney Metal Tool Co.)

A. NOTCHING

B. COPING

Fig. 12-11

Fig. 12-12 Notching angle iron

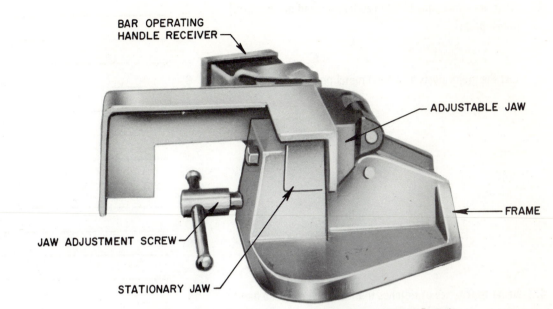

BAR OPERATING
HANDLE RECEIVER

ADJUSTABLE JAW

FRAME

JAW ADJUSTMENT SCREW

STATIONARY JAW

Fig. 12-13 Angle iron bender (Courtesy of The Whitney Metal Tool Co.)

3. Slide the flange to be notched under the blade and align it in the desired position.

4. Close the adjusting block until the angle fits snugly against the blade.

5. Rotate the operating handle clockwise until the blade cuts the notch, figure 12-12.

ANGLE IRON BENDER

The *angle iron bender*, figure 12-13, is a companion tool to the notcher. It is capable of bending angle iron and flat bar in sizes up to a thickness of 1/4 inch and a flange of 2 inches. Any angle of bend can be made. A 32-inch operating bar handle is standard equipment. A heavy-duty machine can be obtained with a capacity of 3 x 3 x 3/8-inch angle iron and 3 x 3/8-inch flat bar.

HOW TO USE THE ANGLE IRON BENDER

1. Notch one flange of the angle iron at the desired bending point.

Fig. 12-14 Angle iron bending

2. Place the unnotched flange in the open jaws of the bender so that the bend mark coincides with the jaw edge. Tighten the jaws.

3. Pull the operating handle to form the desired bend angle, figure 12-14.

SUMMARY REVIEW

A. Place your answers to the following questions in the column to the right.

1. Name the three main parts of the turret punch press.

1. _____

_____

_____

2. What are three shapes that can be punched on the turret punch press?

2. _____

_____

_____

3. List the major parts of a hand metal notcher.

3. _____

_____

_____

_____

_____

_____

_____

_____

_____

_____

4. Name four types of notches that can be made on a hand-operated metal notcher.

4. _____

_____

_____

_____

5. What are the three machines in the angle iron combination machine?

5. _____

_____

_____

B. Insert the correct word or phrase in the following:

1. The _____ indicators on the turrets are used for punch and die alignment.

2. A turret punch press with an 18-inch throat depth will punch a hole in the center of a (an) _____ -inch sheet.

3. To prevent the deadweight fall of the handle and slide on a notcher, the _____ should be checked and tightened if necessary.

4. Piece cutting means starting at the _____ or corner of an inside cut.

5. When using a standard movable shears blade on an angle iron shears, _____ of one leg of the angle iron occurs.

6. The capacity of the turret punch press is _____ -gage mild steel in the _____ punch sizes and _____ for the _____ diameter.

C. Underline the correct word or phrase in the following:

1. A standard angle iron bending machine is capable of bending a flat bar (3/8, 1/4, 1/2, 7/16) inch thick.

2. The operating handle used on the angle iron shears should be (32, 36, 72, 48) inches long.

3. If blades on a notcher are interchanged, the cutting action is called (piecing, splaying, coping, cutting).

4. The standard clearance between the upper and lower blades on the metal notcher is (.05, 1.002, .002, .125) inch.

UNIT 13 SAFETY

OBJECTIVES

After studying this unit, the student will be able to

- List general shop safety rules.

- List the safety rules for the use of power tools.

- Demonstrate the proper and safe use of hand- and power-operated sheet metal tools and machines.

Each sheet metal worker must assume responsibility for the safe operation of any equipment he is using. The worker must maintain and operate any machine in strict conformance with the manufacturer's safety rules and guidelines and those established by the Occupational Safety and Health Act. Accidents in the shop are caused by careless, preoccupied and overconfident people.

GENERAL SAFETY RULES

The following list of rules applies to all machines in the sheet metal shop.

- Before closing the switch to turn on the power to the machine, clean the machine and inspect for loose, worn, damaged, or broken parts. Pay particular attention to the linkage, oil lines, belts, springs, and chains.

- Remove tools and spare machine parts from the working area. Check the tightness of the tooling and attaching parts.

- Check the operating devices and guards to insure proper condition, placement, and adjustment.

- Check the clutch and brake for proper operation.

- During operation, check the machine for overloading.

- Report any questionable operation or unusual action of the machine to the instructor, foreman, or supervisor.

For power-operated machines, the National Safety Council says:

- If it is a moving part . . . color it safe. (Paint moving parts for easy recognition.)

- If there are working handling devices at either end of machine . . . use them.

- If in doubt about a safety procedure . . . read it and heed it.

- If a safety rail is provided on machine . . . grab it.

- If a foot pedal is in use . . . hood it.

- If a foot pedal is not in use . . . lock it.

SAFETY RULES FOR POWER TOOLS

The following safety rules for the use of power tools were developed by the Power Tool Institute, the National Safety Council, Underwriters' Laboratories, and the U.S. Public Health Service.

- *Know your power tool.* Read the instruction manual carefully. Learn the applications and limitations of the machine as well as any potential hazards.

- *Ground all tools unless double insulated.* If a tool is equipped with a three-prong plug, it should be plugged into a three-hole electrical receptacle. If an adapter is used so that a three-prong plug can be inserted into a two-prong receptacle, the adapter wire must be attached to a known ground. Never remove the third prong of the plug.

- *Keep guards in place and in working order.*

- *Keep the work area clean.* Cluttered areas and benches invite accidents.

- *Avoid dangerous environments.* Do not use power tools in damp or wet locations. Make sure the work area has adequate lighting.

- *Keep all visitors away from the work area.*

- *Store unneeded tools.* When not in use, tools should be stored in a dry and high location or in a locked cabinet.

- *Don't force any tool.* A tool will work better and more safely if it is used at the rate for which it is designed.

- *Use the right tool.* Don't force a small tool or attachment to do a job requiring a heavy-duty tool.

- *Wear the proper apparel.* Do not wear loose clothing, long hair, or jewelry near the moving parts of any machinery. Rubber gloves and appropriate footwear are recommended when working outdoors.

- *Use safety glasses with most tools.* In addition, use a face mask if a cutting operation is dusty.

- *Don't abuse the electrical cord.* Never carry a tool by its electrical cord; never yank the cord to remove it from a receptacle. Keep the cord away from excessive heat, oil, and sharp edges.

- *Secure your work.* Use clamps or a vise to hold the work securely. These devices are safer than using your hand to hold the work; both hands are free to operate the tool.

- *Don't overreach.* Keep a proper footing and maintain your balance at all times.

- *Maintain tools with care.* Keep your tools sharp and clean to insure the best possible performance and the most safety in their use. Follow the manufacturer's instructions for lubricating and changing accessories.

- *Disconnect tools.* All power tools must be disconnected from the power source when the tools are not in use, before they are serviced, or when accessories such as blades, bits, or cutters are to be changed.

- *Remove adjusting keys and wrenches.* Always check that keys and adjusting wrenches are removed from the tool before it is turned on.

- *Avoid accidental starts.* When holding or carrying a tool connected to a power source, do not keep your finger on the on-off switch.

STATIONARY POWER-OPERATED MACHINES

Each type of power-operated machine has specially designed safety devices to protect both the operator and the machine. The machine operator must be completely familiar with and understand the operating procedure for the machine and the use of the special safety devices. Through trial and error, the operator must learn the numerous settings and adjustments of the machine for various types and gages of metal. Allowance formulas and other suggested rules are useful as a guide only. Practical allowances are determined on the machine itself.

The following points in general are useful in insuring that new power-driven machinery in any sheet metal shop is used correctly in the most efficient manner.

- A manufacturer's representative may be sent to the sheet metal shop to teach a potential operator how to use new equipment.

- Each adjustment and setup possible on the machine is demonstrated.

- The new operator practices and questions each operation after the demonstration until sufficient skill is developed.

- A helper is assigned to the trained operator who then instructs the helper on the correct procedures of running the machine.

This practice of training operators on the job results in reduced accidents to the operator and prevents costly misuse of the machine. An incorrect setup or an improper adjustment by an unskilled operator can result in personal injury and extensive machine damage.

In addition to the individual instruction, the manufacturer provides to the equipment purchaser a booklet containing assembly drawings of the machine, electrical wiring diagrams, installation procedures, and a list of optional accessories and their application. Written instructions are provided which cover the mechanical and electrical installation procedures, general machine operation, adjustments and controls, and general maintenance and lubrication programs. Cautions regarding machine usage are clearly outlined. A parts replacement list and service recommendations are also provided.

The operation of small power-driven machines such as circle shears, turning machines, and brakes is similar to the procedures outlined in the descriptions of hand-operated machines.

SAFETY AND HEALTH PROTECTION ON THE JOB

The Williams-Steiger Occupational Safety and Health Act of 1970 lists regulations for the safety and health protection of workers on the job. The U.S. Department of Labor, which has primary responsibility for administering the act, issues job safety and health standards. Both employers and employees are required to comply with these standards. By law, safety on the job is the responsibility of everyone!

The Williams-Steiger Act requires that each employer maintain for his employees a working location that is free from recognized hazards which may cause serious injury or death. The act further requires that employers comply with the specific safety and health standards issued by the Department of Labor. The Williams-Steiger Act also requires that each employee comply with the safety and health standards, rules, regulations, and orders issued under the act and applicable to his conduct.

COMPLIANCE WITH SAFETY AND HEALTH REQUIREMENTS

To insure compliance with its safety and health regulations, the U.S. Department of Labor conducts periodic job site inspections by trained safety and health compliance officers. The law requires that an authorized representative of the employer and a representative of the workers be given an opportunity to accompany the inspector to assist in the inspection. Workers also have the right to request an inspection by the Department of Labor if they believe that unsafe and unhealthy conditions exist at their work site. Employees also have the right to bring unsafe conditions to the attention of the safety and health compliance officer making the inspection. If an inspection shows that the act has been violated, the Department of Labor issues to the employer a citation of violation and a proposed penalty. This citation of violation must be displayed prominently at or near the place of violation.

The Williams-Steiger Act provides for mandatory penalties of up to $1,000 for each serious violation; optional penalties of up to $1,000 for each lesser violation also can be placed on an employer. Penalties of up to $1,000 are required for each day during which an employer fails to correct a violation within the period set in the citation. Also, any employer who willfully or repeatedly violates the act is to be assessed civil penalties of not more than $10,000 for each violation.

Criminal penalties are also covered in the act. Any willful violation resulting in the death of an employee for which an employer is convicted, is punishable by a fine of not more than $10,000 or imprisonment for not more than six months, or both. Conviction of an employer after a first conviction doubles these maximum penalties.

The act provides that employees may not be discharged or discriminated against in any way for filing safety and health complaints or otherwise exercising their rights under the act.

SUMMARY REVIEW

A. Place your answers to the following questions in the column to the right.

1. What are two general precautions the worker should take before turning on the power to any machine?

   1. _____
     _____

2. List three safety checks the operator should make of the operating devices and guards on a machine.

   2. _____
     _____
     _____

3. State the eighteen safety rules for power tools as developed by the Power Tool Institute.

   3. _____
     (multiple blank lines)

B. Insert the correct word or phrase in the following:

1. The Williams-Steiger Occupational Safety and Health Act of 1970 provides job _____ and _____ protection for the worker.

2. The primary responsibility for administering the Williams-Steiger Act belongs to the _____ _____ .

3. Under the Williams-Steiger Act, the employer must furnish a place of employment free from _____ _____ .

4. Periodic _____ are conducted by the U.S. Department of Labor.

C. Underline the correct word or phrase in the following:

1. Large power-operated machines do not have special (safety devices, operating instructions, weights).

2. Original demonstrations are carried out on newly purchased equipment by the (shop foreman, superintendent, manufacturer's representative).

3. Operating instructions for large power-operated machines are taught by (lecture, demonstration, reading).

4. Training of operators for large power-operated machines occurs (in the classroom, at the seller's plant, on the job).

UNIT 14 DRILL PRESS

OBJECTIVES

After studying this unit, the student will be able to

- List the parts of a drill press.
- Make any drill press adjustments necessary before drilling.
- List types of drill bits that can be used with the drill press.
- Demonstrate the proper procedures for using the drill press.

The drill press is used for various drilling operations, the most common of which is drilling holes. There are many types of drill presses which all use the same principle of rotating a twist drill by power.

There are a number of tasks to be completed before the drill press can be operated:

- The work must be securely held by some mechanical means.
- The cutting tools must be fastened properly in the spindle.
- The spindle speed must be changed for the particular job.
- The work must be centered on the table under the drill.

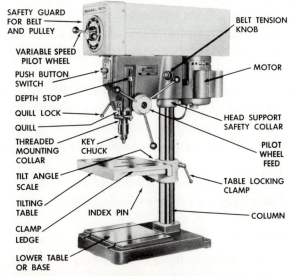

SAFETY GUARD FOR BELT AND PULLEY
VARIABLE SPEED PILOT WHEEL
PUSH BUTTON SWITCH
DEPTH STOP
QUILL LOCK
QUILL
THREADED MOUNTING COLLAR
KEY CHUCK
TILT ANGLE SCALE
TILTING TABLE
INDEX PIN
CLAMP LEDGE
LOWER TABLE OR BASE

BELT TENSION KNOB
MOTOR
HEAD SUPPORT SAFETY COLLAR
PILOT WHEEL FEED
TABLE LOCKING CLAMP
COLUMN

Fig. 14-1 Bench model drill press (Courtesy of the Rockwell Manufacturing Company, Power Tool Division)

- The stop must be adjusted for the depth of the hole to be drilled.

To keep the drill press in the proper operating condition, the sheet metal worker should follow the manufacturer's recommended maintenance and lubrication schedules.

DRILL PRESS

The *sensitive drill press* consists of a base, column, work table, head containing the spindle, belt drive, and motor, figure 14-1.

The *twist drills* are held in a chuck, or sleeve, attached to the spindle. The spindle and chuck are lowered to the work with a hand-feed wheel. The heads of some drill presses can be moved to any position and clamped. The speed of the spindle can be changed by means of a system of pulleys of different sizes connected with a belt. This belt also helps to reduce the vibration of the spindle.

The work is placed on the work table and can be clamped in any position. The adjustable depth stop on the head of the drill press prevents the operator from drilling deeper than necessary.

The sensitive drill press is light in construction. It is designed to operate at high speeds for the drilling of small holes. This type of drill press is called sensitive because of its accurately balanced spindle which enables the operator to feel the cutting action of the drill. In this manner, the operator can judge the amount of pressure necessary to feed the drill into the work.

Fig. 14-2 15" floor model drill press (Courtesy of the Rockwell Manufacturing Company, Power Tool Division)

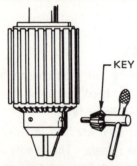

Fig. 14-3 Key-type drill chuck

Fig. 14-4 Reaming with tapered shank reamer (Courtesy of the Rockwell Manufacturing Company, Power Tool Division)

Sensitive drill presses are available either as a bench or a floor model. The bench model has a short column and is intended to be mounted on a bench, figure 14-1. The floor model has a long column so that it can be bolted to the floor, figure 14-2.

Chuck and Key

Drills and other cutting tools used in the sensitive drill press are usually straight-shank tools which are held in a drill *chuck* mounted in the spindle. A number of drill chuck models are available to meet the requirements for light- and medium-duty work. For sensitive drill presses, the chuck will hold drills capable of making holes up to a diameter of 1/2 inch in metal. Holes 5/8 inch in diameter can be drilled in cast iron.

The body of the chuck is fitted with jaws which adjust to fit drill shanks of different sizes. The jaws are opened and closed by means of a *key*, figure 14-3.

Drill Sleeve

Drills and tools with tapered shanks are inserted directly in the drill press spindle, figure 14-4. Drills of different sizes also vary in the size of the shank diameter. To compensate for varying shank sizes, *sleeves* or *sockets* are inserted in the spindle and then the drill is inserted in the sleeve.

A drill press spindle with a tapered hole is shown in figure 14-5A. The sleeve which fits into the tapered hole in the spindle is shown in part B of the figure, and the tapered shank drill which fits into the sleeve is shown at C. Sockets are longer than sleeves but otherwise are similar.

The small ends of the tapered shank drill, sleeve, and socket are all provided with a tang which fits into a slot at the end of the tapered hole in the spindle. Since the taper alone is not sufficient to prevent the drill from slipping, the tang helps to drive the drill.

Some drill chucks have tapered shanks which fit into spindles in a manner similar to drills.

Drill Drift

A drill drift, figure 14-6, is a wedge-shaped tool used to remove a sleeve, socket, or drill from the spindle. Tools are removed from the spindle by forcing the drift into the slot of the sleeve, socket, or spindle.

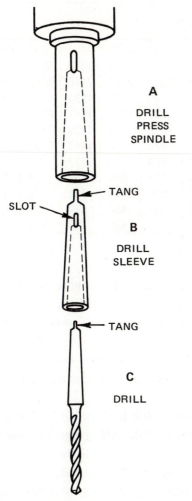

Fig. 14-5 Tapered shank drill and sleeve for spindle

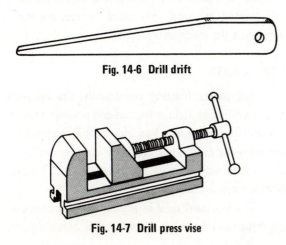

Fig. 14-6 Drill drift

Fig. 14-7 Drill press vise

Drill Press Vise

To obtain satisfactory results when drilling, the work must be held properly. The practice of holding the work on the drill press by hand is discouraged since it usually results in broken drills and may cause injury to the operator. To mount the work properly, the following holding devices are used: drill press vises, C-clamps, or drill jigs.

The *drill press vise* is the most commonly used holding device, figure 14-7. Vises of this type usually are constructed with a movable jaw operated by a screw. The vise should be used for materials which will not spring when the jaws are tightened.

The speed of the spindle in revolutions per minute (abbreviated rpm) must be adjusted for the size of the drill used. The speed is changed by adjusting the stepped pulleys of the drill press. The rpm range of the spindle is usually marked on the head of the drill press.

Tables 14-1 and 14-2 indicate the correct spindle speed settings for high-speed drills of various diameters. Table 14-1 indicates the recommended

Suggested Speeds for High Speed Steel Drills

	Speed in S.F.M.
Alloy Steel. . . . . 300 to 400 Brinnel . . .	20-30
Stainless Steel	30-40
Automotive Steel Forgings	40-50
Tool Steel, 1.2C	50-60
Steel .4C to .5C	70-80
Mild Machinery Steel, .2 to .3C	80-110
Hard Chilled Cast Iron	30-40
Medium Hard Cast Iron	70-100
Soft Cast Iron	100-150
Malleable Iron	80-90
Monel Metal	40-50
High Tensile Strength Bronze	70-150
Ordinary Brass and Bronze	200-300
Aluminum and its alloys	200-300
Magnesium and its alloys	250-400
Slate, Marble and Stone	15-25
Bakelite and similar material	100-150
Wood	300-400

Table 14-1

Table of Cutting Speeds (Fraction Size Drills)

Feet per Min.	30'	40'	50'	60'	70'	80'	90'	100'	110'	120'	130'	140'	150'
Diameter Inches	Revolutions per Minute												
1/16	1833	2445	3056	3667	4278	4889	5500	6111	6722	7334	7945	8556	9167
1/8	917	1222	1528	1833	2139	2445	2750	3056	3361	3667	3973	4278	4584
3/16	611	815	1019	1222	1426	1630	1833	2037	2241	2445	2648	2852	3056
1/4	458	611	764	917	1070	1222	1375	1528	1681	1833	1986	2139	2292
5/16	367	489	611	733	856	978	1100	1222	1345	1467	1589	1711	1833
3/8	306	407	509	611	713	815	917	1019	1120	1222	1324	1426	1528
7/16	262	349	437	524	611	698	786	873	960	1048	1135	1222	1316
1/2	229	306	382	458	535	611	688	764	840	917	993	1070	1146
5/8	183	244	306	367	428	489	550	611	672	733	794	856	917
3/4	153	203	255	306	357	407	458	509	560	611	662	713	764
7/8	131	175	218	262	306	349	393	436	480	524	568	611	655
1	115	153	191	229	267	306	344	382	420	458	497	535	573

Table 14-2

Material	Lubricant
Aluminum and its alloys:	Soluble oil; kerosene and lard oil compounds; light, nonviscous, neutral oil; kerosene and soluble oil mixtures.
Brass:	Dry; soluble oil; kerosene and lard oil compounds; light, nonviscous, neutral oil.
Copper:	Soluble oil; winter-strained lard oil; oleic acid compounds.
Cast Iron:	Dry, or with a jet of compressed air for a cooling medium.
Malleable Iron:	Soluble oil, or nonviscous, neutral oil.
Monel Metal:	Soluble oil, or sulfurized mineral oil.
Steel, Ordinary:	Soluble oil; sulfurized oil; high Extreme Pressure value mineral oil.
Steel, vary hard and refractory:	Soluble oil; sulfurized oil; turpentine.
Steel, Stainless:	Soluble oil, or sulfurized mineral oil.
Wrought Iron:	Soluble oil; sulfurized oil; high animal oil content, mineral oil compound.

Table 14-3 Lubricants

speed in surface feet per minute (sfm) for different materials. Table 14-2 indicates the allowable spindle speed in rpm for drills of various sizes for specified sfm values.

The speeds at which carbon steel drills can be used are 40 to 50 percent of the speeds given in table 14-2.

If the drill is rotated at too fast a speed, then the corners of the cutting edges will wear too rapidly. If the drill is fed too quickly into the material, the cutting edges will chip or break.

Speed changes on modern drill presses, figures 14-1 and 14-2, are made only while the machine is running. On older model drill presses where the belts are changed by hand, any speed changes are made only while the machine is stopped.

LUBRICANTS

Lubricants (cutting compounds) are required during drilling to reduce friction and prevent a rise in the drill temperature. Too high a drill temperature will burn the drill. Lubricants also improve the finish of the work and increase the life of the drill by preventing excessive wear.

The lubricant used in any situation depends on the type and hardness of the metal being drilled.

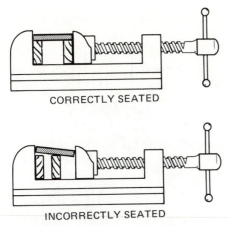

CORRECTLY SEATED

INCORRECTLY SEATED

Fig. 14-8 Work seated on parallels

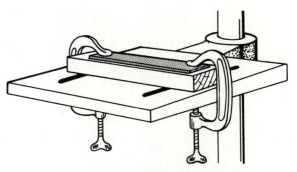

Fig. 14-9 Holding work with C-clamps

When drilling low carbon steel the recommended lubricants used are lard oil or a soluble cutting compound such as a mixture of a soluble oil and water. The operator must apply the lubricant to the work and drill with a brush or an oil can. Table 14-3 shows the recommended lubricants for drilling different materials.

DRILL SIZES

There are four systems of designating drill sizes: fractional, number, letter, and metric. In the fractional system, the drills vary in size by fractions of an inch; in the letter or number systems, a letter or number represents a definite decimal size; and in the metric system, drill sizes are given in millimeters.

The drill size is marked on the shank of small, straight-shanked drills and on the recess between the body and the shank of larger drills. The size of a drill can be measured with a micrometer or a drill gage. A drill gage has holes which correspond to drill sizes.

HOW TO DRILL SMALL HOLES

1. Select a vise and parallel bars or a hardwood block. A vise is used to hold materials which will not spring when the jaws are tightened. Parallel bars are used for accurate work.

2. Grip the work in the vise so that the area of the hole to be drilled is between the jaws of the vise. To prevent the drill from going into the

base of the vise, the work is placed on the block or on the parallels as shown in figure 14-8.

3. Seat the work by tapping it with a lead mallet.

4. Slide the vise and work under the drill so that the center of the hole to be drilled is located over the center of the worktable of the drill.

5. Fasten the vise securely to the table with clamp straps or place a stop in close contact with the vise to prevent it from turning. If a vise is not used, clamp the work and a wood block to the worktable with C-clamps. In this case also, the work is clamped so that the hole to be drilled is located near the center of the worktable, figure 14-9. This latter method of securing the work is used when drilling light metal.

6. Select a drill of the proper size.

   If the drill press is provided with a drill chuck, straight shank drills must be used. For taper shank drills with shank tapers smaller than the spindle taper, the correct sleeve or socket size must be selected and inserted in the spindle before the drill can be installed.

7. Remove all dirt and metal chips from the shank of the drill, the sleeve or socket, and the spindle hole. Check the shanks of the tools for burrs which will cause the drill to run out of true. All burrs and abrasions should be removed carefully with a file or oilstone.

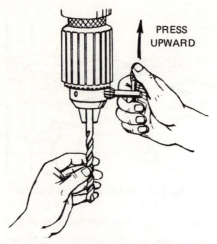

Fig. 14-10   Chucking the drill

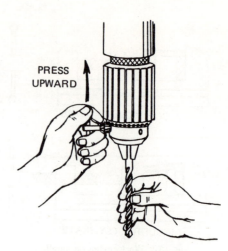

Fig. 14-11   Removing the drill

8. Insert the drill in the chuck and tighten the jaws of the chuck with the key. Figure 14-10 shows the proper method of chucking a drill. The correct method of removing the drill is shown in figure 14-11. If the operator presses up on the key while turning it, there is less wear on the teeth of the chuck.

If a drill with a tapered shank is to be used, insert the shank of the drill in the spindle and insure that the tang end of the shank is aligned with the slot, figure 14-12. Use a sleeve or socket if necessary to adapt the shank to the taper of the spindle. The sleeve or socket is secured in the spindle by tapping it with a lead mallet.

9. Turn on the power momentarily to check that the drill runs true.

CAUTION   The key or drift must not be left in the chuck or slot.

10. Adjust the worktable so that the work is slightly under the level of the top of the drill. Tighten the clamping screw.

For the majority of upright drill presses, both vertical and horizontal adjustments of the worktable are secured by tightening the same clamping screw. Thus, in these cases, the clamping screw is not tightened until after the horizontal adjustment is made.

11. Adjust the table in the horizontal direction by swinging it either to the right or to the left, to

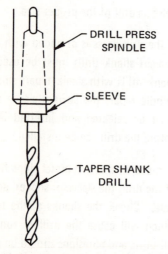

- DRILL PRESS SPINDLE
- SLEEVE
- TAPER SHANK DRILL

Fig. 14-12   Sleeve and drill mounted in spindle

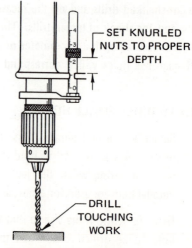

- SET KNURLED NUTS TO PROPER DEPTH
- DRILL TOUCHING WORK

Fig. 14-13   Setting the stop

align the location of the hole to be drilled with the point of the drill. Tighten the clamping screw.

Some drills and sensitive drill presses are not provided with a horizontal adjustment for the worktable. For these machines, the work and the holding device must be placed in the desired position on the worktable.

12. Adjust the spindle speed with the variable speed pilot wheel. Refer to tables 14-1 and 14-2 for the proper cutting speed in rpm for the drill size being used.

13. Set the adjustable stop for the required depth of the hole or thickness of the metal, figure 14-13.

14. Start the machine and feed the drill slowly until the point is started in the metal. Raise the drill and check to see that the drill is started in the proper location. If the location of the drill is not correct, relocate the hole with a center punch.

15. Lower the drill to the work; feed the drill to the required depth.

16. Remove and clean the drill.

SUMMARY REVIEW

A. Place your answers to the following questions in the column to the right.

1. Name the major parts of the sensitive drill press.

1. _____
_____
_____
_____
_____
_____
_____
_____

2. Name two devices that hold a drill bit in the drill press spindle.

2. _____
_____

HOW TO DRILL SHEET METAL

The main difficulties the sheet metal worker may have when drilling sheet metal are:

- The drill is not rigidly held in the line of feed.
- Excessive feed pressure causes deformation in the metal before the actual cutting begins.
- The metal deforms and work hardening occurs.
- An improper drill size is selected.

To overcome these difficulties, the sheet metal worker should follow the procedure below.

1. Locate the center of the hole on the sheet metal; mark the center with a scratch awl or prick punch.

2. Select a drill with short flutes and a heavy web construction. If this type of drill is not available, use a standard drill and cut off about one-third of the flute; then resharpen the drill.

3. Place the metal on a wood block, align it with the drill point, and use clamps to secure the metal and block to the table.

4. Start the drill and feed steadily until the desired depth is reached.

CAUTION Never hold sheet metal with your hand when drilling. Serious accidents can result.

3. List three methods of holding material for drilling in the drill press.

3. _____
    _____
    _____

4. List two reasons why a backup piece of wood is used in drilling sheet metal.

4. _____
    _____

5. List the four systems used to designate drill bit sizes.

5. _____
    _____
    _____
    _____

B. Insert the correct word or phrase in the following:

1. The principle by which the drill press operates is the rotation of a (an) _____ by power.

2. Straight shank twist drills are held in a drill _____ which is mounted in the _____

3. Tapered shank twist drills are held directly in the drill press _____ .

4. The purpose of a (an) _____ on the small end of a tapered shank twist drill is to prevent _____ .

5. Drills can be removed with a (an) _____ or _____ .

C. Underline the correct word or phrase in the following:

1. Work should be held for drilling on the drill press with the (hand, pliers, drill press vise).

2. Too fast a drill speed will result in danger to the (job, cutting edges of the drill, drill press).

3. When drilling low carbon steel, the drill should be lubricated with (kerosene, neutral oil, lard oil).

4. Drill sizes are marked on the (flute, web, shank) of the drill.

5. (Burrs, numbers, flutes) on a drill shank will cause the drill to run out of true.

UNIT 15 GRINDER

OBJECTIVES

After studying this unit, the student will be able to

- Name the parts of the grinder.
- List the hand tools that can be sharpened on a grinder.
- Properly mount a grinding wheel and dress it.
- Demonstrate the proper procedures in using a grinding wheel.

Grinding is the process of removing material by the cutting action of abrasive particles coating a revolving grinding wheel. The particles cut as they come into contact with the surface to be ground.

Grinding machines are available in numerous types and sizes to satisfy a variety of grinding requirements. A motor-driven bench or floor grinder is the type commonly used for hand grinding, figures 15-1 and 15-2.

A roughing grinding wheel coated with coarse abrasive particles is usually mounted on one end of the spindle and a finishing wheel with finer abrasive particles is mounted on the other end. Tools may be held and steadied on the toolrest during grinding. The toolrest can be adjusted horizontally and vertically and then locked in place.

Cast iron wheel guards with integral dust chutes are provided on the grinder to protect the operator from flying abrasive particles and ground material. Shatterproof glass shields also provide protection.

Hand grinders are used for all types of general grinding and for sharpening prick punches, center punches, chisels, drills, and other small tools. The larger sizes of grinders are commonly used for grinding welds and heavy castings.

HOW TO OPERATE A GRINDER

1. Examine the grinder to see that the toolrest is: (a) set at the required height (usually 1/4 to 1/2 inch below the center of the wheel); (b) close

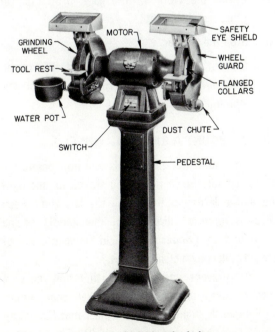

Fig. 15-1 10" Pedestal grinder

Fig. 15-2 7" Standard bench grinder

(Courtesy of the Rockwell Manufacturing Company, Power Tool Division)

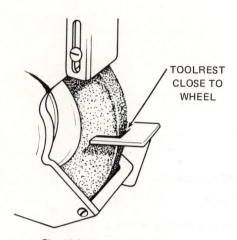

Fig. 15-3 Toolrest in position

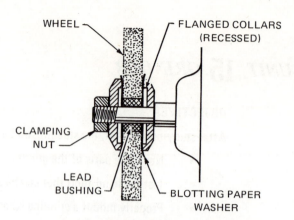

Fig. 15-4 Mounting a wheel on a straight spindle

to the face of the wheel (not more than 1/8 inch away) (c) securely fastened, figure 15-3.

2. Adjust the glass shields so that they provide both a clear view of the work area and protection to the operator from flying particles.

CAUTION   Wear safety goggles if the grinder is not equipped with glass shields.

3. Start the grinder and stand to one side of the grinding wheels during the grinding operation. The toolrest should not be adjusted while the grinder is running.

  Note: Excessive vibration of the grinder means something is wrong. Stop the grinder immediately and examine the machine and the grinding wheels thoroughly.

4. Place the work on the toolrest. Hold the work in the right hand and steady it with the left hand. Guide the work against the face of the revolving wheel and apply enough pressure to achieve a cutting action. This pressure will vary due to the hardness of the material and the wheel. In general, the work should be supported on the toolrest to steady it when grinding. For small tool bits, however, support them in the left hand and rest this hand on the toolrest.

CAUTION   Keep your fingers away from the revolving wheel, especially when grinding small pieces.

5. The work normally will heat up during the grinding process. To prevent the work from burning or losing its temper (becoming soft), cool the work in water.

6. Grind the job to the required shape or size by moving the work back and forth across the face of the wheel. This back and forth movement results in a more even surface on the work and prevents the wearing of a groove in the wheel.

  Remove as much metal by rough grinding as possible; use the finer wheel for finishing. Do not grind on the side of the wheel.

7. Check the work with a gage, protractor, or other measuring tool.

8. Stop the grinder.

  Do not use the grinder to grind thin metal. Never grind soft materials such as copper, solder, aluminum, or babbit.

HOW TO MOUNT A GRINDING WHEEL

To insure that the wheels will not loosen, the grinder spindle has a right-hand thread on the right end and a left-hand thread on the left end. Each wheel is mounted directly on the spindle of the bench or floor grinder and is held between a pair of flanged collars by a clamping nut.

To prevent undue strains that may cause a wheel to break, great care must be used when mounting the wheels, figure 15-4. A wheel that fits tightly should never be forced on the spindle. The fit of the

A. STAR-TYPE DRESSER

B. DIAMOND POINT DRESSER

Fig. 15-5 Grinding wheel dressers

Fig. 15-6 Dressing a grinding wheel with a diamond point
(Courtesy of the Rockwell Manufacturing Company, Power Tool Division)

wheel can be changed by scraping or filing the lead bushing in the wheel mounting hole until the wheel slips freely on the spindle.

The sheet metal worker must always place blotting paper washers or pads of a soft compressible material between the sides of the wheel and the flanged collars. The addition of these pads lessens the danger of strains being set up in the wheel. The clamping nut should be drawn tightly against the flanged collar to prevent the wheel from turning on the spindle. After mounting the wheel, check it for trueness and balance. Replace all guards before starting the grinder. Use only wheels which are the correct size for the grinder. The wheels are marked with an rpm rating. New or oversize wheels may break apart if improperly matched to the grinder.

HOW TO DRESS A GRINDING WHEEL

Dressing is the process of restoring the sharpness of the grinding wheel either by breaking away the dulled abrasive crystals or by removing the glazed (loaded) surface of the wheel. In either case, new, sharp abrasive grain cutting edges are exposed on the surface of the wheel

If the proper wheel is used for the job, the abrasive crystals should wear away just fast enough to cause sharp cutting edges to be exposed to the job. However, since the standard bench grinder may be used for many different jobs, the wheel must be dressed periodically.

The dressing process is not the same as *truing*. Truing is the process of shaping any part of the wheel to alter it to some desired shape.

The tools used for dressing are called *dressers*. The more commonly used dressers are shown in figure 15-5: a star-type dresser in 15-5A and a diamond point dresser in 15-5B.

To dress the wheel, support the dresser on the toolrest so that the point of contact of the tool is slightly above the center of the wheel. The handle of the dresser is tilted upward as shown in figure 15-6.

Gradually press the dresser against the face of the revolving wheel until it *bites*, that is, until it makes contact with the wheel surface. Move the dresser back and forth on the wheel so that a straight surface is achieved. At the same time, hold the dresser rigidly enough on the toolrest to insure trueness.

CAUTION The dressing tool should be held with a firm grip to prevent accidents.

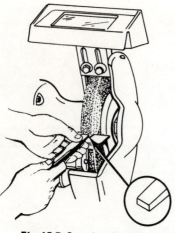

Fig. 15-7 Squaring the chisel

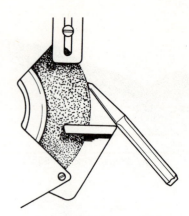

Fig. 15-8 Chisel at proper angle

HOW TO GRIND A COLD CHISEL

1. To square the chisel, hold the chisel on the toolrest at right angles to the wheel, figure 15-7. Press the chisel against the face of the revolving wheel and move it back and forth across the face. Continue this movement until the nicks are removed from the chisel and any broken corners are ground square.

2. To grind the cutting edge of the chisel, hold the chisel at the angle shown in figure 15-8 and support it with the left hand.

3. Press the edge of the cold chisel against the face of the revolving wheel and move the edge in an arc back and forth across the face of the grinding wheel. Keep the body of the chisel at the

same point on the toolrest, figure 15-9. This procedure is called *swinging*.

The chisel should be cooled in water periodically to prevent it from overheating and drawing the temper.

4. Repeat step 3 for the cutting edge on the other side of the chisel. Using a protractor with a swinging arm, check the point for the proper angle.

5. To remove any burrs, lightly press the side of the chisel against the face of the wheel, figure 15-10.

HOW TO GRIND A PRICK PUNCH OR CENTER PUNCH

The point of a center punch is ground to an angle of about 90 degrees; the point of the prick

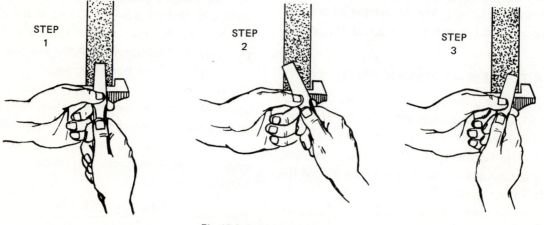

Fig. 15-9 Swinging the chisel

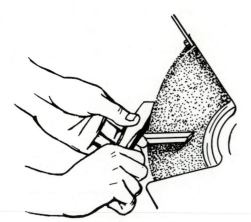

Fig. 15-10 Removing burrs

Fig. 15-12 Sharpening a prick punch

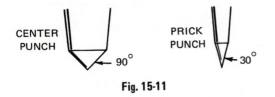

CENTER PUNCH   90°

PRICK PUNCH   30°

Fig. 15-11

punch is ground to an angle of about 30 degrees, figure 15-11.

1. Hold the punch at the proper angle with the right hand and support it with the left hand.

2. Press the point of the punch against the face of the revolving wheel. Move the point back and forth across the face of the wheel. At the same time, rotate the punch with the fingers of the right hand, figure 15-12. Cool the punch in water from time to time to prevent it from overheating and drawing the temper.

3. Sharpen the point on an oilstone.

HOW TO SHARPEN A TWIST DRILL

1. Adjust the toolrest to the horizontal position, figure 15-13.

2. Scribe 59-degree lines on the face of the toolrest as guides, figure 15-14A.

3. Align one cutting lip of the drill on a 59-degree line on the toolrest and press the drill against the grinding wheel.

4. When the lip of the drill contacts the wheel, raise the cutting edge of the drill and lower the

Fig. 15-13 Sharpening a twist drill (Courtesy of the Rockwell Manufacturing Company, Power Tool Division)

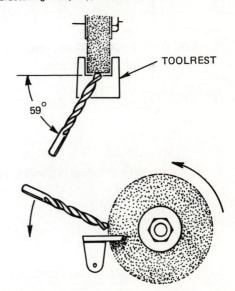

TOOLREST

59°

Fig. 15-14 Twist drill aligned with 59-degree guide on toolrest

shank end while slightly rotating the drill, figure 15-14B.

5. Repeat steps 1 to 4 for the opposite cutting edge.

CAUTION

Keep the cutting edge on a horizontal plane. Cool the drill frequently with water. Keep the drill point centered.

SUMMARY REVIEW

A. Place your answers to the following questions in the column to the right.

1. Name the parts of a floor or bench model grinder.

1. _____
_____
_____
_____
_____
_____
_____
_____

2. Name three types of hand tools that can be sharpened on the 7-inch bench grinder.

2. _____
_____
_____

3. List three precautions that an operator should take before starting a grinder.

3. _____
_____
_____
_____
_____

4. List three precautions to take regarding the toolrest before the grinder is operated.

4. _____
_____
_____
_____
_____

5. List three steps to follow in grinding a chisel.

5. _____
_____
_____
_____

6. Name two commonly used grinding wheel dressers.

6. _____
_____

B. Insert the correct word(s) or phrase in the following:

1. The toolrest can be adjusted _____ and _____ and then locked _____ in place.

2. Safety eye glass shields should be adjusted to permit a(an) _____ of the work and still protect the operator.

3. Never adjust the _____ while the grinder is running.

4. When grinding small pieces, keep your _____ away from the wheel.

5. When grinding, remove as much metal as possible on the _____ wheel and finish on the _____ wheel.

6. Always use the _____ wheel for the grinder.

7. Dressing restores the _____ of the grinding wheel.

C. Underline the correct word or phrase in the following:

1. To prevent damage to a tool during grinding, it should be cooled in (oil, water, benzene).

2. The center punch should be ground to an included angle of (30, 60, 90) degrees.

3. When sharpening a cold chisel, the edge should be moved across the face of the wheel (in a straight line, at an angle, in an arc).

4. When dressing a wheel, the dresser is moved (vertically, stands stationary, horizontally, back and forth).

5. If the fit of the wheel is snug when it is being mounted on the grinder, (tap it with a hammer, tighten the clamping nut with a large wrench, scrape out the lead bushing).

6. A grinding wheel can be used to remove material from (copper, aluminum, steel) objects.

7. Do not use a grinder to grind (cast iron, stainless steel, any thin metal).

UNIT 16 PITTSBURGH LOCKFORMER, BUTTON PUNCH SNAP LOCK MACHINE, POWER FLANGER, AND BAND SAW

OBJECTIVES

After studying this unit, the student will be able to

- List the major parts of the lockformer, button punch snap lock machine, flanger, and band saw.

- List the operations possible with these machines.

- Adjust and use each machine properly.

LOCKFORMER

The *lockformer*, figure 16-1, uses two rolls to form a variety of edges and seams. The type of edge or seam is determined by the set of rolls selected. Figure 16-2 shows the rolls that can be used on the lockformer, the resulting seam or edge, the capacity of each pair of rolls, the approximate amount of material used, and the size of the seam.

In general, lockformers are factory set to make two types of seams, usually the Pittsburgh lock and the double seam. The task of changing the rolls to make other types of seams or angle flanges is a difficult and time-consuming job. As a result, many sheet metal shops find it more economical to use a machine with the factory settings for the standard seams and several other machines for other types of seams.

The lockforming machines can accommodate sheets 7 inches and longer. If shorter sheets are needed, a long piece can be notched and then cut later.

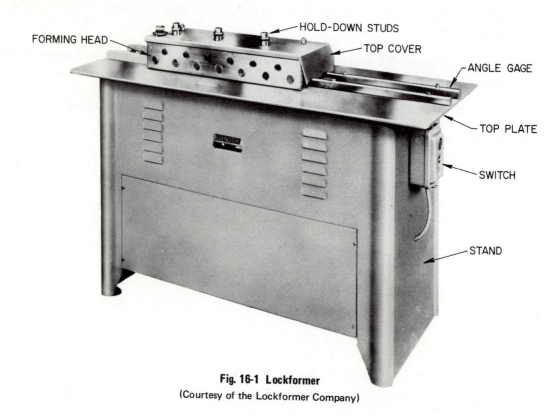

Fig. 16-1 Lockformer
(Courtesy of the Lockformer Company)

STANDARD AUXILIARY ROLLS MOUNTED ON OUTBOARD SHAFTS

	ROLLS	CAPACITY (gage)	APPROX. MATERIAL USED	SIZE
	Pittsburgh Lock Rolls, 5/16" Pocket	22 to 28	1"	5/16" Pocket
	Double Seam Rolls (Type S)	22 to 28	1 1/8"	3/8" Seam
	Double Seam Rolls (Type L)	16 to 22	1 1/4"	7/16" Seam
	Drive Cleat Rolls	20 to 26	2 1/8"	1 1/8" Width
	Standing Seam Rolls	16 to 20	2 1/8"	3/4" Height
	Right Angle Flange Rolls	16 to 24	———	up to 7/16" High
	Combination 3-in-1 Rolls with Special Guide — Right Angle Flange	22 to 26	———	1/2" Height
	Standing Seam	22 to 26	———	5/8" Seam
	T-Connection	22 to 26	———	5/8" Seam

Fig. 16-2

Hold-down adjustments are necessary if the material slips, tends to leave the gage, or curls up at the finish of the forming operation.

HOW TO ADJUST THE HOLD-DOWN

1. Remove the top cover of the lockformer.

2. Tighten the hold-down studs until they are snug; then loosen the studs a quarter turn. This setting usually gives the proper adjustment for all thicknesses of material.

3. If the material slips, tighten the studs equally until the material stops slipping.

4. If the material curls up after leaving the forming head, or if it shows extremely heavy pressure marks, loosen the studs slightly.

If a wider or narrower hammer-over edge is required, the angle gage on the right-hand side of the lockformer can be moved to the desired width. When moving the gage, keep it parallel to the front edge of the top plate of the machine. Never move the left-hand angle gage of the lockformer.

Care

Six alemite fittings are located on the underside of the standard roller case. Since these fittings lubricate the main reduction bearings, they should be lubricated after every four hours of operation with a standard viscous lubricant. The gears should be greased periodically. Clean the rolls at regular intervals using a compressed air hose to blow out chips and flakes.

HOW TO USE THE LOCKFORMER

1. Lay out the sheet metal for the required size of the seam or flange.

2. Add the seam allowances given in figure 16-2.

3. Cut the piece to size. Remove any burrs and straighten the metal if it is twisted.

4. Hold the metal against the angle gage and slide it into the forming head. Hold the metal against the gage until the seam or flange is completely formed.

BUTTON SNAP LOCK MACHINE

The *button snap lock machine* is a lockformer equipped with a special set of rolls for forming a button snap lock, figure 16-3. This machine is designed for manufacturing commercial and industrial duct-work from metal ranging in thickness from 20 to 24

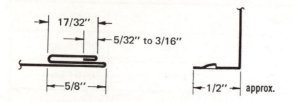

Fig. 16-3 Button snap lock

Fig. 16-4 Button snap lock machine
(Courtesy of the Lockformer Company)

Fig. 16-5 Automatic power flanger

gage. The button snap lock machine produces both the receiver lock and the button-punched right angle flange.

Smaller button snap lock machines for 24- to 30-gage material are available for small shops.

This type of machine has several advantages: it forms a foolproof, permanent lock which is always located at the corner of the square duct; there is no hammer-over edge; hand tools are not required.

The approximate amount of material used to make a button snap lock is 1 3/4 inches for metal thicknesses of 20 to 24 gage and 1 9/16 inches for metal thicknesses of 24 to 30 gage.

HOW TO USE THE BUTTON PUNCH SNAP LOCK MACHINE

1. Lay out the pattern size including the seam allowance for the size of the machine to be used.

2. Cut the sheet to the pattern size.

3. Feed the sheet into the forming head; hold the edge of the sheet against the angle guide until the edge is formed, figure 16-4.

POWER FLANGER

The automatic *power flanger*, figure 16-5, may be purchased as an attachment for the lockforming machine or as a self-powered, portable or bench-mounted machine.

Machines are available with capacities of 16 gage to 24 gage and 18 gage to 26 gage. The flange height for the 16- to 24-gage machine is 3/8 inch; for the 18- to 26-gage machine the flange height is 1/4 inch. A minimum radius of 3 1/4 inches can be flanged.

ADJUSTMENTS

Metal Thickness

To adjust for the thickness of the metal to be flanged, tighten the adjusting screw on the front of the block of the machine, figure 16-6A. The screw should be tightened completely and then loosened

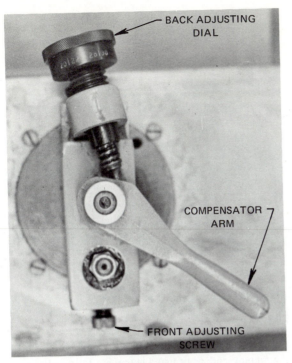

BACK ADJUSTING DIAL

COMPENSATOR ARM

FRONT ADJUSTING SCREW

Fig. 16-6A Flanger

Fig. 16-6B Starting of flange in notch

approximately one-eighth of a turn. (This setting is usually correct for 26-gage material.) The front gage adjusting screw should be just tight enough to draw the material through the rolls. If the front gage adjusting screw is too tight, the material will be stretched and wrinkled.

Spring Tension

To obtain the proper spring tension on the compensator arm, the adjusting dial on the back side of the flanger is adjusted to the stop. Tighten the adjusting dial and then turn it back to the proper gage setting shown on the adjusting dial. The spring tension is necessary if the compensator arm is to guide the material through the rolls automatically at the proper rate.

HOW TO USE THE POWER FLANGER

1. Insert the leading edge of the work to be flanged in the slot in the table; bend the work away from the operator approximately 45 degrees, figure 16-6B.

2. Start the leading edge of the material into the rolls. If the material pulls at the rolls, either

the front adjusting screw is too loose or the back adjusting dial is not tight enough.

Note: When starting a partially formed section that contains an inside curve, push the compensator arm back until it locks out of position. Feed the partially formed section into the rolls. The machine will pull the material through the rolls. As the unformed portion of the material approaches the rolls, bring the compensator arm forward until it contacts the material. Hold the compensator arm so that the spring tension is not applied to the piece until the unformed section comes to the rolls; apply pressure to the piece until the flange picks up and then release the compensator arm so that automatic guiding is resumed.

BAND SAW

Two types of band saws are used in modern sheet metal shops. For the *vertical saw*, figure 16-7, page 114, the blade travels in a vertical plane; in the

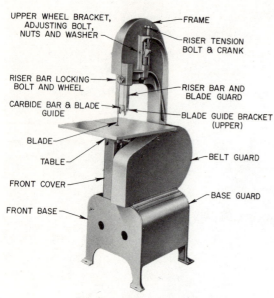

UPPER WHEEL BRACKET, ADJUSTING BOLT, NUTS AND WASHER
FRAME
RISER TENSION BOLT & CRANK
RISER BAR LOCKING BOLT AND WHEEL
RISER BAR AND BLADE GUARD
CARBIDE BAR & BLADE GUIDE
BLADE GUIDE BRACKET (UPPER)
BLADE
TABLE
BELT GUARD
FRONT COVER
BASE GUARD
FRONT BASE

Fig. 16-7 Vertical band saw

Fig. 16-8 Horizontal band saw

horizontal saw, figure 16-8, the blade travels in a horizontal plane. Of the two types, the vertical band saw is considered to be the most useful in the sheet metal shop.

Both types of band saws have three blade speeds: 100, 600, and 3000 fpm. The speeds are controlled by a V-belt drive on pulleys of various sizes. The blade wheels are flanged so that the wheel will not slip off while the machine is running. In addition, quick, easy blade changes are possible with the flanged wheels. All band saw bearings are ball bearings with neoprene seals; lubrication of these bearings is unnecessary.

Blades

The saw blade will have a longer cutting life if the recommendations listed below are followed:

1. Do not twist the blade.

2. Blade teeth should always point downward.

3. Keep at least three teeth in the work at all times to prevent breakage.

4. Be sure the blade teeth clear the outside slot of the guide blocks.

5. Feed the work into the blade using constant pressure.

The recommended minimum cutting radii for blades of various sizes are: 1/8-inch blade, 1/8-inch

CUTTING RECOMMENDATIONS

Galvanized Sheets	26-gage stock, 1 to 50 sheets, 14- to 32-pitch blade	600 fpm
Steel Sheets	Hot rolled, cold rolled, metal types other than galvanized, 14- to 32-pitch blade	100 fpm
Aluminum Sheets	Stack of 15 to 30 or more, 4-pitch blade; single sheet, 24-pitch blade; lubricate the blade with beeswax or cutting oil.	600 fpm
Stainless Steel Sheets	Single sheet only to 12 gage, 14- or 24-pitch blade; friction cut, dull or sharp blade	3000 fpm

radius; 3/16-inch blade, 5/16-inch radius; 1/4-inch blade, 5/8-inch radius; 3/8-inch blade, 1 7/16-inch radius; and 1/2-inch blade, 2 1/2-inch radius.

BLADE ADJUSTMENT

1. Place the blade on the rubber tires of both the upper and lower wheels; the back edge of the blade should rest against the flanges of both wheels.

2. Increase the tension on the blade by turning the riser bolt clockwise (to the right). Do not put the blade under heavy tension.

3. By hand, slowly revolve the wheels forward.

CAUTION   Never adjust any part of the saw while the motor is running.

4. If the blade creeps away from the upper wheel flange, turn the upper wheel bracket adjusting bolt to tilt the upper wheel in slightly at the top.

5. When the blade tracks against the flanges, lock the adjusting nut.

BLADE GUIDE ADJUSTMENT

1. Adjust the upper and lower blade guide brackets so that the slit in each carbide thrust and blade guide is parallel and centered with the blade.

2. Move the upper and lower carbide thrust and blade guides in and out, so that the back of the blade clears the back of the slot in the carbide guides by about 1/64 inch.

3. When the blade runs freely through both blade guides, lock the guides into position by tightening the Allen setscrew.

HOW TO USE THE BAND SAW

1. Scribe the cutting line on the material surface.

2. When the saw is adjusted and running, place the piece to be cut on the table and line up the starting edge with the saw blade.

3. Feed the piece into the saw blade with a steady pressure; guide the piece so that it follows the cutting line.

SUMMARY REVIEW

A.   Place your answers to the following questions in the column to the right.

1. List the parts of the lockformer.

1. _____
_____
_____
_____
_____
_____
_____
_____

2. Name the types of seams and locks that can be made with a lockformer.

2. _____
_____
_____
_____

3. What are the advantages of the button snap lock forming machine?

3. _____
_____
_____
_____
_____
_____

4. List the parts of the power flanger.

4. _____

_____

_____

_____

5. Name the five major parts of the band saw as shown in figure 16-7, page 114.

5. _____

_____

_____

_____

_____

B. Insert the correct word or phrase in the following:

1. Changing the rolls on a lockformer is _____ and _____ -consuming.

2. Lockformers are made to accommodate sheets _____ and longer.

3. If the material slips when passing through the lockformer, the _____ should be tightened.

4. Never move the _____ angle gage on the lockformer.

5. The main reduction bearings on the lockformer should be _____ after every four hours of operation.

6. The button snap lock machine produces the _____ lock and the button-punched right angle.

7. The power flanger is available as a (an) _____ to the lockformer.

8. If the front gage adjusting screw on the power flanger is too tight, the material will _____ and _____ .

9. The leading edge of the work must be _____ at a 45-degree angle before it is fed into the power flanger.

10. Both _____ and _____ band saws are used in the shop.

C. Underline the correct word or phrase in the following:

1. Band saws are driven by belts that can be arranged to give (1, 2, 3) different blade speeds.

2. To keep the blades from slipping off, the blade wheels on a band saw have (screws, bolts, flanges).

3. The teeth on the band saw blade must always point (up, down, out, in).

4. A blade on a band saw should always have (1, 2, 3) or more teeth in contact with the work.

5. The minimum cutting radius for a 1/4-inch wide band saw blade is (1/8, 5/16, 5/8, 1 7/16) inch(es).

6. If a wider hammer-over edge is desired on the lockformer, the (right-hand, left-hand, angle) gage is adjusted.

7. The approximate amount of material used by the button snap lock machine on 26-gage galvanized iron is (1 3/4, 1 5/16, 1 9/16, 1 1/2) inches.

8. The heavy-gage power flanger will flange to a height of (3/16, 1/4, 5/16, 3/8) inch.

9. The lockformer is factory set to make (drive cleats, right angle flanges, standing seams, Pittsburgh locks).

UNIT 17 ELECTRIC DRILL, SCREWDRIVER, GRINDER, AND SANDER-GRINDER

OBJECTIVES

After studying this unit, the student will be able to

- List the precautions to be followed to insure the safe operation of power-driven hand tools.

- List the uses for each tool.

- Demonstrate the proper method of operating each tool.

All portable power-operated tools are energized by an electric current. The electric current drives an electric motor which is the heart of the tool. The motor converts the electrical energy to mechanical energy which does the work for which the tool is intended. The sheet metal worker *must always* follow certain precautions in the use of power-driven tools to prevent the possibility of a shock. An *electric shock* is the passage of an electric current through an individual's body to the ground to complete an electrical circuit. It is necessary to check that:

- The tool is grounded properly with a third wire.

- The cord and tool are properly insulated.

- The operator is not in contact with wet or damp ground.

- The operator is not in contact with an outside source of current.

- The cord is not crimped.

For proper operation, electric tools require a constant line voltage as specified on the nameplate of the tool. A low line voltage will cause a decrease in the speed of the tool and a high line voltage will increase the speed. In both cases, the tool will heat up quickly. Excessive heat will damage the tool. The value of the line voltage supply should be compared with the rating on the nameplate of the tool to insure that they are compatible. As the distance between the point of use of the tool and the source of power increases, extension cables must be used. The conductor wires of the extension cables must be of the correct size so that a constant line voltage is maintained. Table 17-1 is a guide to the correct wire size for tools operated at varying distances from the

Table 17-1

Full Load Amperes	0	2.1	3.5	5.1	7.1	12.0
Rating of Tool Amperes	2.0	3.4	5.0	7.0	12.0	16.0
Distance in Feet	Wire Size (B & S Gage)					
25	18	18	18	18	16	14
50	18	18	18	16	14	12
75	18	18	16	14	12	10
100	18	16	14	12	10	8
200	16	14	12	10	8	6
300	14	12	10	8	6	4
400	12	10	8	6	4	4
500	12	10	8	6	4	2
600	10	8	6	4	2	2
800	10	8	6	4	2	1
1000	8	6	4	2	1	0

Example: What size conductors are recommended if a portable electric sander rated at 110 volts, 7.0 amperes is to be operated 100 feet from the source of power?

Answer: No. 12 conductors.

Note: For 220-volt tools, use a wire size corresponding to a length equal to 1/2 the actual length.

power source. The recommended wire sizes are based on 150 percent of the full tool load and a loss of not over 5 volts in the line for 110-volt tools.

ELECTRIC DRILL

One of the most useful power-driven tools is the *electric drill*, figure 17-1. Both standard general-purpose and heavy-duty drills are available. Both types of drills can be obtained with chucks sized to hold 1/4-, 3/8-, or 1/2-inch drills. Single speed and variable speed electric drills are available.

Trigger speed controls are mounted in the drill handle. There are three types of drill handles: in-line grip, pistol grip, and side grip. For variable speed drills, the speed can be controlled from zero rpm to the maximum rpm rating of the drill. Some drills have reversible motors controlled by a switch located below the trigger switch.

All drills have heat-treated, helical alloy steel gears and hardened shafts with Jacob's-geared, key-type chucks. The following accessories may be added to any type of drill: right-angle drive unit, grinding wheel, wire wheel brush, cloth buffing wheel, or extension shanks.

HOW TO USE AN ELECTRIC DRILL

A. *Variable Speed Drill*

1. Mark the center of the hole to be drilled. Center punching is not necessary.

2. Tighten the drill bit in the chuck with a key.

3. Place the drill point on the center of the hole to be drilled. Hold the drill bit at a 90-degree angle to the surface to be drilled.

4. Start the drill at a slow speed. Exert a slight pressure on the drill until the center location is secured.

5. Increase the drill speed and apply forward pressure until the hole is drilled.

B. *Single Speed Drill*

1. Mark the center of the hole to be drilled and center punch the location.

2. Tighten the drill bit in the chuck with a key.

3. Hold the drill bit at a 90-degree angle to the surface to be drilled with the drill point on the center punch mark.

4. Press the trigger switch of the drill on and off until the hole center is secured.

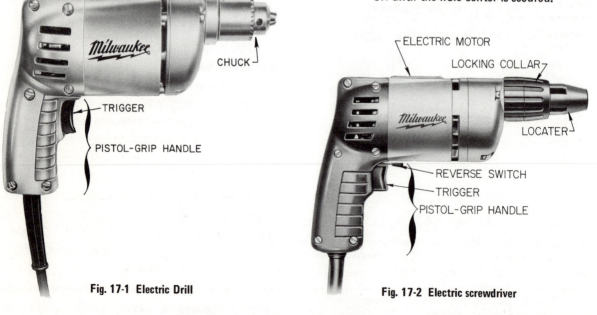

MOTOR UNIT

CHUCK

TRIGGER

PISTOL-GRIP HANDLE

ELECTRIC MOTOR

LOCKING COLLAR

LOCATER

REVERSE SWITCH

TRIGGER

PISTOL-GRIP HANDLE

Fig. 17-1 Electric Drill

Fig. 17-2 Electric screwdriver

(Courtesy of Milwaukee Electric Tool Corporation)

Locater for washer
head screws

Standard Locater

Locater for Magnetic
Bit Holders

Locater for corrugated
metal and restricted areas

Fig. 17-3 Locaters for electric screwdriver

5. Press and hold the trigger switch on and apply forward pressure to the drill until the hole is drilled.

CAUTION

Never try to hold a turning chuck.
Remove the chuck key before starting the drill.
Turn the drill off immediately if the bit starts to bind in the material.
Avoid excessive pressure.

ELECTRIC SCREWDRIVER

The electric screwdriver, figure 17-2, is designed to drive self-drilling, self-tapping fasteners in steel, brass, bronze, aluminum, and stainless steel. The screwdriver also is used for fastening wood or other compressible materials to metal.

The safety precautions given for the use of an electric drill also apply to the use of an electric screwdriver.

This tool has a positive clutch that engages when pressure is applied; the clutch stops the driving action when the pressure on the tool is released or when the locater contacts the work surface.

The electric screwdriver is provided with either an in-line handle or a pistol-grip handle. A trigger switch is located in the handle. A reversing switch is mounted above the trigger switch. When the reversing switch is pushed to the left, the screwdriver bit will rotate clockwise; pushed to the right, counterclockwise rotation results.

An electric screwdriver will drive self-drilling, self-tapping screws up to a size of 1/4 inch in cold rolled steel to a maximum material thickness of 3/16 inch. Standard accessories for this tool consist of interchangeable locater sleeves, socket head extensions, an insert bit holder, and numbers 2 and 3 Phillips screwdriver bits. Other accessories are available. Fig-

ure 17-3 illustrates several types of accessory locater sleeves.

Locater sleeves are changed by pulling the locking collar back toward the tool housing and unscrewing the collar. Then the proper sleeve is inserted and the collar is retightened and replaced in its correct position.

DEPTH CONTROL ADJUSTMENT

Electric screwdrivers are provided with a depth adjustment to control the depth to which a screw can be driven. The adjustment is made using the following procedure.

1. Pull the locking collar back toward the motor housing.

2. Rotate the locater sleeve clockwise to increase the depth allowance. Rotate the sleeve counterclockwise to decrease the depth allowance. Each notch on the locater sleeve represents 1/64 inch of travel.

3. Release the locking collar at the desired setting. The projections on the collar must engage the notches in the locater sleeve.

The electric screwdriver lubrication performed at the factory will last for six months to one year depending on the amount of use. Long tool life depends on a regular schedule for lubrication and brush and commutator inspection.

HOW TO USE THE ELECTRIC SCREWDRIVER

1. Select and install the proper locater.

2. Place the screw head in the locater.

3. Place the point of the screw at the proper location on the material.

4. Turn on the power and exert a forward pressure on the screwdriver.

Fig. 17-4 Sander-grinder

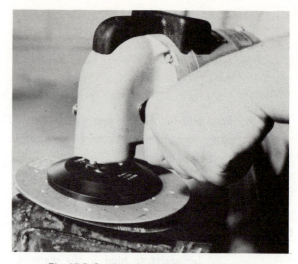

Fig. 17-5 Sander-grinder held at proper angle

5. Release the pressure when the locater strikes the material surface.

A starting hole is not required in light-gage metals; a pilot hole is required for heavy-gage metals.

SANDER-GRINDER

When using the *sander-grinder* shown in figure 17-4, the sheet metal technician must follow the safety precautions outlined for the use of all power-operated tools. In addition, the technician must:

- *Wear goggles for all abrasive sanding operations.*

- *Never use the spindle button lock as a brake.*

- *Switch the tool to off before unplugging it.*

- *Never place the tool on the face of the disc when it is not in operation.*

The electric sander-grinder has a 115-volt, 60-Hz, 5000 rpm, 1 1/2-horsepower motor which drives the operating discs (usually 7 or 9 inches in diameter). The tool is equipped with a spring-loaded clutch drive to assure smooth operation. The clutch drive also prevents harmful backlash when a heavy or unbalanced grinding wheel is attached to the tool.

The parts of the tool are the button-type spindle lock, removable side handle, heavy-duty urethane tool-rest, large fan, lightweight aluminum alloy housing, external brush holders, double-pole dustproof switch, ball bearing-mounted rotor assembly, and rotor and stator windings.

Steel backing pads are provided on the sander-grinder to serve as a support for the following accessories: flared cup grinding wheels, wire cup brushes, flat reinforced grinding discs, and abrasive sanding discs.

HOW TO INSTALL GRINDING OR SANDING DISCS

1. Place the tool on its toolrest with the spindle upright.

2. Place the grinding or sanding pad on the steel backing pad.

3. Slip the disc nut through the arbor hole in the abrasive disc and hub assembly.

4. Tighten the disc nut by turning it clockwise.

5. Depress the spindle lock button with one hand and turn the pad to the right with the other hand until the pad engages and locks.

6. Tighten the pad as much as possible.

HOW TO USE THE SANDER-GRINDER

1. Grasp the rear and side handles firmly.

Fig. 17-6 Portable grinder
(Courtesy of Milwaukee Electric Tool Corporation)

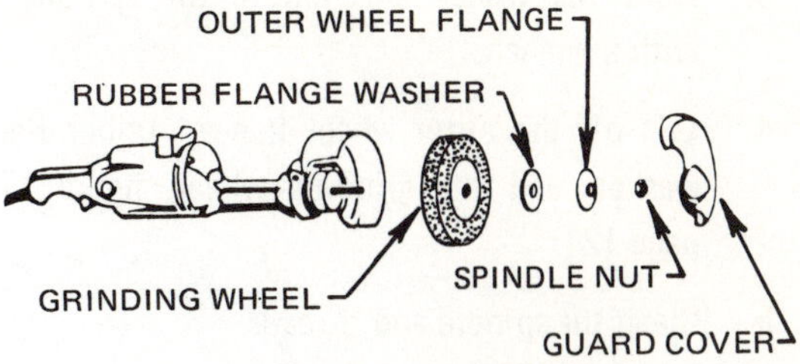

Fig. 17-7 Grinding wheel mounting

2. Move the tool from side to side across the material using long sweeping strokes.

3. Hold the sander-grinder at a 5- to 10-degree angle, figure 17-5.

4. Use a coarse disc to remove ridges from the material.

5. Use a fine disc (80 grit for steel) for final finishing.

6. The sander-grinder strokes for the final finish should be made at right angles to the direction of the coarse finish.

CAUTION:

- Heavy pressure on the tool causes irregular patterns.

- A bumpy surface results if the angle at which the tool is held is too flat (less than 5 degrees).

- Too coarse a disc causes circular grinding marks and deep scratches on the material. A partially glazed disc and dirt, loose metal, or loose grit either on the disc or the material being sanded will cause deep scratches in the material.

- Slow movements, circular motion, or excessive pressure will give rise to excessive heat and a bluish discoloration.

- Too great a pressure at the end of a stroke causes flat areas and low spots.

Fig. 17-8 Using a portable disc grinder
(Courtesy of Milwaukee Electric Tool Corporation)

PORTABLE GRINDER

The portable grinder, figure 17-6, is available with 4-, 5-, or 6-inch grinding wheels. It is driven by a 115-volt, 60-Hz, 4000-6000 rpm motor. It is factory lubricated for an initial operating period of 2 to 6 months, depending upon the amount of use. The portable grinder has a lightweight aluminum alloy housing, an adjustable shatterproof steel guard, an enclosed dustproof switch, helical alloy steel gears and shaft, and oversize ball bearings. Commonly used accessories are the crimped wire brush and the cloth buffing wheel.

HOW TO MOUNT GRINDING WHEELS

1. Disconnect the tool from the electrical outlet.

2. Remove the wheel guard cover by removing the screws at the top of the cover.

3. Hold the wheel and remove the spindle nut with a wrench.

4. Lift off the outer wheel flange, rubber flange washer, and the grinding wheel, figure 17-7, page 121.

5. Clean the spindle and threads.

6. Replace the grinding wheel, rubber flange washer, and the outer wheel flange.

7. Replace and tighten the spindle nut.

8. Replace the guard cover and fasten it securely.

9. Run the grinder at full speed for about a minute.

HOW TO USE THE PORTABLE GRINDER

1. Grasp the grinder firmly, figure 17-8, page 121. Allow the motor to reach full speed.

2. Apply the wheel to the work gradually.

3. The grinder may be used with the wheel held parallel to the work or the wheel may be placed at an angle to the work.

CAUTION

- Never use the side of the wheel for grinding.
- If the grinder begins to bind on the material, remove it immediately.
- Never use a damaged or badly worn wheel.

SUMMARY REVIEW

A. Place your answers to the following questions in the column to the right.

1. List the five precautions an operator should take when using an electric power tool.

    1. _____
       _____
       _____
       _____
       _____
       _____

2. What are three types of handles used on electric drills?

    2. _____
       _____
       _____

3. List three different operations that can be accomplished with the electric drill.

    3. _____
       _____
       _____

4. List five metals into which self-drilling, self-tapping fasteners can be driven using the electric screwdriver.

    4. _____
       _____
       _____
       _____
       _____

5. List the parts of the sander-grinder.

    5. _____
       _____
       _____

_____

_____

_____

_____

_____

_____

6. Name the two common accessories used on the electric   6. _____
    grinder.
                                                                    _____

                                                                    _____

B. Insert the correct word or phrase in the following:

1. When using electric power tools, _____ energy is converted to _____ energy.

2. An _____ is the passage of an electric current through a person's _____
    to the _____ .

3. Too _____ or too _____ a line voltage will cause the electric tool to _____
    up quickly.

4. The _____ the extension cord the greater the _____ drop.

5. The speed of the electric power drill is controlled by means of a _____ .

6. When using a variable speed drill, the center of the hole to be drilled does _____ have to
    be center punched.

C. Underline the correct word or phrase in the following:

1. A drill is held at a (45, 60, 90)-degree angle to the surface to be drilled.

2. A drill should be started at a (slow, fast, medium) speed until the center location is secured.

3. The capacity of the electric screwdriver is (1/8, 3/16, 1/4)-inch, self-drilling, self-tapping screws in
    3/16-inch cold rolled steel.

4. When using the electric grinder or sander, always wear (gloves, goggles, long sleeve shirts).

5. Too great a pressure on the electric sander-grinder will cause (marks, deep marks, deep scratches,
    irregular patterns) on the material.

6. Never use a (badly worn, new, circular) wheel on the electric grinder.

UNIT 18 ELECTRIC SHEARS, NIBBLER, AND RECIPROCATING SAW

OBJECTIVES

After studying this unit, the student will be able to

- List the major parts of the electric shears, nibbler, and reciprocating saw.
- List the uses for these tools.
- Operate each tool properly.

ELECTRIC SHEARS

The *electric shears*, figure 18-1, is designed to operate on 115 volts, 50-60 Hz. The precautions outlined in the previous unit for the use of electric power tools must be followed. Do not operate any power tool in a gaseous or explosive atmosphere. Keep the motor clean by occasionally blowing out any foreign matter with an air hose.

The electric shears has a capacity of 16-gage mild steel and 17-gage stainless steel. For left-hand shears, the cutting radius is a minimum of 1/2 inch; the cutting radius is a minimum of 1 inch for right-hand shears. Blade clearance is factory set for cutting 16-gage cold rolled steel. The use of the proper blade clearance will result in longer blade life and cleaner edges.

Clearance Adjustment

To adjust the lower blade for a horizontal gap or clearance, use a socket wrench to loosen the lower blade clamping screw, figure 18-1. Turn the positioning screw in or out to increase or decrease the gap. Measure the gap with a feeler gage. Recommended gap sizes are .010 inch for 14-gage material, .008 inch for 16 gage, .006 inch for 18 gage, .004 inch for 20 gage, and .002 inch for material lighter than 20 gage. When the clearance is correct, tighten the blade clamping screw.

For all cutting operations, the forward edge of the upper blade should be 3/32 inch from the lower blade when the ram is at the bottom of its stroke, figure 18-2. To measure this gap, move the ram to its lowest position by adjusting the positioning screw of the ram with a socket wrench.

If adjustment or replacement of the upper blade is necessary, remove the upper blade clamping screw so that the blade falls free and exposes the upper blade backup screw. Raise or lower the backup

RAM POSITIONING SCREW

MILWAUKEE

LOWER BLADE

UPPER BLADE CLAMPING SCREW

UPPER BLADE

BLADE POSITIONING SCREW

YOKE

BLADE CLAMPING SCREW

Fig. 18-1 Electric shears

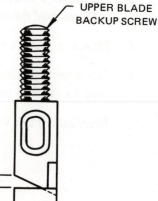

UPPER BLADE BACKUP SCREW

3/32"

Fig. 18-2

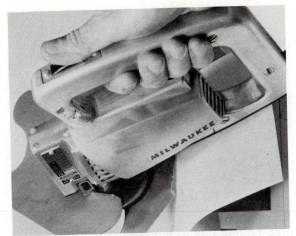

Fig. 18-3 Cutting with electric shears

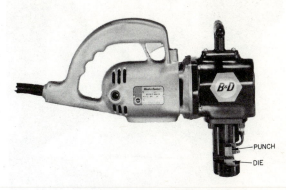

Fig. 18-4 Electric nibbler

screw with a socket wrench until the desired vertical setting is achieved. Each turn of the screw changes the setting 1/32 inch. Replace the blade and the upper blade clamping screw in their correct locations.

HOW TO USE THE ELECTRIC SHEARS

1. Lay out the cutting line on the sheet metal to be cut.

2. Hold the shears so that the waste portion of the metal is to the right of the shears, figure 18-3.

3. With the shears turned on, start at the edge of the material and follow the cutting line.

4. Keep the back of the shears as low as possible.

5. Use an even forward pressure.

    Note: Excess pressure causes the tool to jam. Burrs result if the back of the shears is held too high. Waste to the left of the shears causes metal distortion and a rough edge on the cut piece.

ELECTRIC NIBBLER

The *electric nibbler*, figure 18-4, will cut many types of sheet metal up to a thickness of 8 gage. It will also cut corrugated metal, plastics, composition materials, and stainless steel up to a thickness of 10 gage.

The nibbler operates on a punch-and-die principle. As the tool is fed along the cutting line, small rectangular pieces are punched out leaving a smooth edge. The material on either side of the cutting line is not distorted. An automatic lubrication device deposits the proper amount of oil on the work as the cut progresses. The oil increases the life of the punch and die. The combination of a heat-treated and nitrided high-speed steel punch and a carbide die develops a pressure equal to that of a two-ton punch press.

The electric nibbler is factory lubricated; the oil reservoir should be filled periodically with a good grade of machine oil. The nibbler has an outside cutting edge radius of 3 3/8 inches and an inside cutting edge radius of 3 3/32 inches.

HOW TO USE THE NIBBLER

1. Lay out the cutting line on the material. If both pieces of the material are to be used, make an allowance for the width of the punch cut.

2. Grasp the tool firmly with one hand on the rear in-line handle. Hold the work with the other hand.

3. Start the cut at the edge of the sheet and follow the cutting line until the cut is complete, figure 18-5, page 124.

Rest the bottom of the tool on the table. If the tool can not be supported on a table, attach an overhead spring line to the front tee handle. If two hands are used on the tool, the piece being cut should be held in a brake or clamped to the table.

Fig. 18-5 Cutting with nibbler

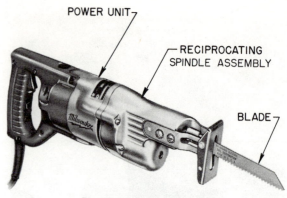

Fig. 18-6 Reciprocating saw

RECIPROCATING SAW

The *reciprocating saw,* figure 18-6, is an electrically-operated tool and thus the safety rules previously outlined must be followed.

The reciprocating saw is powered by a 115-volt, 60-Hz motor. For this tool, the rotary motion of the motor is converted to the reciprocating motion of the blade. Three types of saws are available; for all general work, a single-speed saw with a speed of 2250 strokes per minute; for specific cutting requirements, a two-speed saw with speeds of 1700 and 2400 strokes per minute; and a variable speed saw with a speed range of 1100 to 2250 strokes per minute. Seventeen types of blades are available for cutting any shape in wood, plaster, metal, plastics, masonite, builder's transite, and other materials.

The reciprocating saw is lubricated at the factory; the saw will require additional lubrication every six to twelve months depending on the amount of use it receives. Periodic inspection and cleaning of the motor brushes and commutator is recommended.

HOW TO USE THE RECIPROCATING SAW

Installing the Blade

1. Select the proper blade for the material to be cut.

2. Loosen the socket head screw on the blade clamp.

3. Slide the blade under the pin-type blade clamp so that the pin is seated in the blade tang hole.

4. Tighten the socket head screw.

Cutting Resilient Materials

1. Position the saw on the material as in figure 18-7A.

2. Apply pressure and lower the blade into the work using the shoe as a pivot, figure 18-7B.

3. As the blade cuts, raise the handle until the shoe rests firmly on the work, figure 18-7C.

4. Continue the cut until it is complete.

Cutting Metal

1. In light-gage metal, use a sharp chisel to cut a starting hole. In metal with a thickness of 18

Fig. 18-7 Cutting resilient materials with the reciprocating saw

gage or greater, use a drill to make the starting hole.

2. Place the blade in the starting hole and cut the desired shape. Use low saw speeds for cutting hard materials and higher speeds for soft materials.

Hold the shoe firmly against the work to minimize the transfer of vibration to the operator.

Offset Cutting Using the Offset Blade Adapter

1. Remove the socket head screw and the blade clamp.

2. Place the adapter over a spindle and line up the hole in the adapter casting with the threaded hole in the spindle.

3. Replace the socket head screw to attach the adapter to the spindle.

4. Secure the blade as in steps 1 to 4 of the procedure for installing the blade.

5. Make the cut using the procedures outlined for cutting either resilient materials or metals.

SUMMARY REVIEW

A. Place your answers to the following questions in the column to the right.

1. List the adjustable parts of the electric shears.

1. _____

2. Name the two principal parts of the nibbler.

2. _____

3. What are some of the materials that can be cut with a nibbler?

3. _____

4. List the three principal parts of a reciprocating saw.

4. _____

5. List six materials that can be cut with various types of reciprocating saw blades.

5. _____

B. Insert the correct word or phrase in the following:

1. The capacity of the electric shears is _____ gage for mild steel and _____ gage for stainless steel.

2. For all cutting operations using the electric shears, the forward edge of the _____ blade should be set _____ from the _____ blade.

3. Excess pressure applied when using the electric shears will cause the tool to _____

4. The nibbler operates on the _____ and _____ principle.

5. The electric nibbler _____ out small rectangular pieces and leaves _____ edges on the material.

6. The reciprocating saw converts _____ motion of the _____ to _____ motion of the saw blade.

7. When using a reciprocating saw, _____ speeds are used for _____ materials and _____ speeds are used for _____ materials.

C. Underline the correct word or phrase in the following:

1. When cutting with a reciprocating saw, hold the shoe firmly against the work to prevent (breaking the blade, an irregular cut, shock or vibration transfer).

2. An electric shears can cut a minimum left-hand radius of (5/16, 1/4, 1/2) inch.

3. The factory setting of the blades on the electric shears is for (10, 14, 16, 18)-gage mild steel.

4. A nibbler will cut sheet metal up to a thickness of (16, 18, 10, 8) gage.

5. The minimum outside cutting radius for a nibbler is (3 3/32, 2 1/2, 3 3/8) inches.

UNIT 19 *PITTSBURGH LOCK HAMMER, ROTARY HAMMER, AND ELECTRIC HAMMER*

OBJECTIVES

After studying this unit, the student will be able to

- List the uses of the Pittsburgh lock hammer, rotary hammer, and electric hammer.
- Demonstrate the proper use of each tool.

PITTSBURGH LOCK HAMMER

The *Pittsburgh lock hammer*, figure 19-1, is designed to provide a rapid and neat method of closing seams. The closing rate is up to 20 feet per minute depending on the type and thickness of the metal.

The Pittsburgh lock hammer can be used with sheet metal ranging in thickness from 30 gage to 22 gage. The hammer is powered by a 115-volt, ac/dc motor. The motor should be checked from time to time for brush and commutator wear. Dirt can be removed from the commutator while the motor is running using sandpaper. The screws on the external housing of the hammer should be checked periodically for tightness since they may be loosened by the vibration of the tool when in use. The Pittsburgh lock hammer is factory lubricated; do not overgrease the hammer as this may damage the tool.

HOW TO USE THE PITTSBURGH LOCK HAMMER

1. Form the edges of the metal to be joined in the usual manner, figure 19-2.

2. Position the edges to be locked and tack down each end with a tacking hammer. A few extra tacks along the length of the edge are advisable.

   If there is any obstruction in the material, tack down the area about an inch before the obstruction with a smaller hammer.

3. Place the lock hammer on the work with the shoe of the hammer on the starting lip of the edge.

Fig. 19-1 Pittsburgh lock hammer

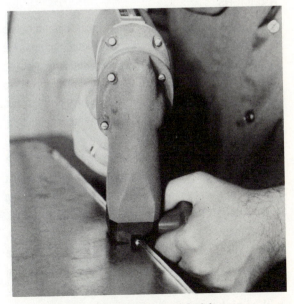

Fig. 19-2 Using the Pittsburgh lock hammer

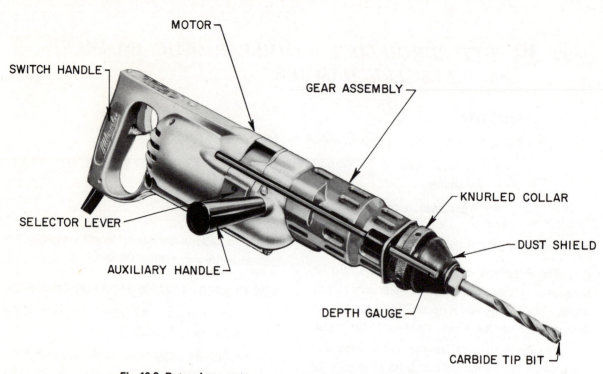

Fig. 19-3 Rotary hammer (Courtesy of Milwaukee Electric Tool Corporation)

4. Pull the trigger switch and slide the tool along the full length of the edge.

5. Exert a slight pressure against the side of the shoe. Hold the hammer in a vertical position at all times.

HAMMERS

Several other types of electric hammers are used by construction workers. These include the hammer-drill, the rotary hammer, and the electric hammer. All of these tools enable the worker to make holes in concrete and masonry structures. The tools also are used for chiseling, channeling, scaling, and slotting.

In addition to the electrical precautions to be followed for power-operated tools, the operator must wear safety glasses and a dust mask when working with materials that give rise to a large amount of dust. The construction worker must grip the tool firmly, never drill through steel reinforcements with carbide bits, check all external housing screws for loosening due to vibration, and blow out the motor frequently with an air hose.

ROTARY HAMMER

The *rotary hammer*, figure 19-3, is used with tapered carbide-tip hammer bits ranging in size from 1/4 to 7/8 inch in diameter. A Jacobs chuck can be adapted to this tool for drilling only. Never use the tool with the Jacobs chuck in place as a hammer as this will permanently damage the chuck. The rotary hammer is factory lubricated. It should be greased after several months use under normal conditions, or if it has been out of use for a prolonged period. Do not overgrease. Inspect and grease the tool by removing the slotted screw in the side gear assembly housing.

The major parts of the rotary hammer are illustrated in figure 19-3. Accessories for self-drilling anchors are available. For some rotary hammer models, core bit adapters, hammer tools, and adapters for scaling, chiseling, slotting and channeling are available. A selector lever on the side of the tool permits the selection of a drilling action only, or a combination of drilling and hammering. For drilling, the selector is turned until the arrow points to the nose of the tool. In this position, pressure must be applied to the bit to initiate the drilling action; this pressure must be firm or the bit will wander.

A dust shield should be used at all times. Contamination of the grease in the machine with dust may cause damage to the tool. When drilling, water should not be used to cool the bit or settle the dust as it will cause permanent damage to the bit.

HOW TO USE THE ROTARY HAMMER

1. Mark the center of the hole to be drilled on the masonry surface.

2. Check the position of the drill bit and set the depth gage.

3. Hold the bit on the center location at a 90-degree angle to the surface to be drilled.

4. Click the switch on and off until the hole center is secured.

5. Run the rotary hammer steadily and exert a firm pressure until the desired depth is reached.

ELECTRIC HAMMER

The *electric hammer*, figure 19-4, has a maximum operating diameter of 1 1/8 inch. For the most efficient use of the tool, however, the operating limit should range from a diameter of 11/64 inch to 7/8 inch.

The general safety precautions outlined for the use of electric tools as well as the special precautions given for the rotary hammer should be followed when using this tool.

The drill bit of this tool does not rotate. Instead, the tool delivers hammer blows in the forward direction, resulting from a simple, direct spring and cam mechanism. A cushioned recoil mechanism eliminates any jolting action.

The mechanism of the electric hammer must be greased prior to each use and again after every hour

Fig. 19-4 Removing bricks with electric hammer

of continuous operation. The tool can not be harmed by overgreasing. The gear case is factory lubricated. The lubrication should be sufficient for a year or longer, depending on the amount of use of the tool.

HOW TO USE THE ELECTRIC HAMMER AS A DRILL

1. Position the tool at the hole location.

2. Exert a firm downward or forward pressure. Insufficient pressure will allow the tool to rebound and wander.

3. Pull the trigger switch and drill the hole. Never allow the tool to run on idle; running the tool without exerting pressure will damage the nose bushing of the tool.

HOW TO USE STAR AND MACHINE DRILLS IN THE ELECTRIC HAMMER

1. Insert a chuck in the nose bushing.

2. Insert the drill shank in the chuck.

3. When hammering, use the chuck side handle to move the drill forward and backward steadily, at a rate of about 30 times per minute.

SUMMARY REVIEW

A. Place your answers to the following questions in the column to the right.

 1. Name the major parts of the rotary hammer.

1. _____

 _____

 _____

 _____

_____ _____

_____ _____

2. List the types of operations that can be accomplished with a rotary hammer.

2. _____

_____

_____

_____

_____

_____

3. List three types of electric hammers used by construction workers.

3. _____

_____

_____

4. List two safety precautions, other than electrical precautions, that the operator of a rotary hammer should take when drilling masonry.

4. _____

_____

_____

B. Insert the correct word or phrase in the following:

1. The Pittsburgh lock hammer is used to _____ seams _____ and _____ .

2. The Pittsburgh hammer should be held in a _____ position.

3. When operating a rotary hammer, the worker must _____ the tool.

4. Never use a hammering action with a(an) _____ installed.

5. Some rotary hammer models may be provided with adapters for _____ bits and _____ tools.

6. To initiate the _____ action of a rotary hammer, _____ must be applied.

C. Underline the correct word or phrase in the following:

1. The capacity of the Pittsburgh lock hammer is (10, 18, 22, 26) gage.

2. When using a rotary hammer, the (Jacobs chuck, dust shield, high speed bit) should always be used.

3. A cold water lubricant on the carbide drill bit of a rotary hammer will (cool, temper, damage) the bit.

4. The bit on the electric hammer is operated by a (rotating action, hammer blow, combination action).

5. If the electric hammer is allowed to idle, (bushing damage, grease contamination, bit damage) will occur.

ACKNOWLEDGMENTS

Publications Director — Alan N. Knofla

Source Editor — Marjorie A. Bruce

Director of Manufacturing / Production — Frederick Sharer

Illustrators — Anthony Canabush, George Dowse, Michael Kokernak

Production Specialists — Jean LeMorta, Sharon Lynch, Patti Manuli, Betty Michelfelder,
Lee St. Onge

The instructional material presented in SMMP has been tested and verified with numerous classes of students at The Washburne Trade School, Chicago, Ill.

The author and the publisher would like to express their appreciation to the following companies for their assistance in providing illustrations and technical information for this text.

The Black & Decker Manufacturing Company — 18-4, 18-5

Di-Acro Division, Houdaille Industries, Inc. — 6-1, 6-2, 6-3, 6-4, 6-5, 6-6, 6-7, 6-8, 6-9, 6-10, 6-11, 6-12, 6-13, 6-14

Dreis & Krump Manufacturing Co. — 7-1, 7-2, 7-3, 7-4, 7-5, 7-12, 7-15, 7-16, 8-1, 8-3, 8-4, 8-5, 8-6, 8-7, 8-8, 8-9, 8-10, 8-12, 8-13, 8-14, 8-15, 8-16, 8-17

The Lockformer Company — 11-3, 16-1, 16-4

Milwaukee Electric Tool Corporation — 17-1, 17-2, 17-6, 17-8, 18-1, 18-3, 18-6, 19-1, 19-3, 19-4

The Peck, Stow & Wilcox Co. — 1-1, 1-2, 1-3, 1-4, 1-8, 2-1, 2-3, 3-1, 3-2, 4-1, 5-1, 5-4, 9-1, 10-1, 11-4, 11-7, 11-8, 12-3, 12-6

Rockwell Manufacturing Company (Power Tool Division) — 14-1, 14-2, 14-4, 15-1, 15-2, 15-6, 15-13, 16-8

Rotex Punch Company, Inc. — 12-1, 12-2

Whitney Metal Tool Co. — 1-9, 12-7, 12-10, 12-13